248.4

DATE DUE

How to Make

L✿fe Work

Michelle McKinney Hammond

How to Make Life Work

The Guide to
Getting It Together and Keeping It Together

FaithWords

NEW YORK BOSTON NASHVILLE

FaithWords
Hachette Book Group USA
237 Park Avenue
New York, NY 10017

Visit our Web site at www.faithwords.com.

Printed in the United States of America

Illustrations by Trish Cramblet
First Edition: March 2008
10 9 8 7 6 5 4 3 2 1

FaithWords is a division of Hachette Book Group USA, Inc.
The FaithWords name and logo is a trademark of Hachette Book Group USA, Inc.

Library of Congress Cataloging-in-Publication Data

McKinney Hammond, Michelle, 1957–
How to make life work : the guide to getting it together and keeping it together /
Michelle McKinney Hammond. —1st ed.
p. cm.
ISBN-13: 978-0-446-58062-5
ISBN-10: 0-446-58062-7
1. Christian life. I. Title.
BV4501.3.M371 2008
248.4—dc22
2007034402

To the Alpha and Omega, The Designer and Sustainer of Life:
In You I move, breathe, and have my very being.
I live for You.

To my loving parents,
Mr. and Mrs. William McKinney and Mr. George Hammond:
I feel doubly blessed to have you. Thank you for showing me
how to make life work.

Contents

Contents

Acknowledgments

Well, Miss Holly, we've done it again! What a trooper you are, O Great Master Editor! Thanks for making me look good and sound sane. Anne, thanks for your patience. Thanks to Brynn and all the team at FaithWords and Hachette who work so hard to make it all happen. Ben, you are so bad (in a good way)! Beth, thanks for always being the calm voice of reason in the midst of absolute chaos!

Thanks to all my friends and family who not only supported me through my struggle to birth this but also put up with being ignored far too long as I wrestled to get this on paper. I love you. It's your turn.

Introduction: Own Your Contribution

We often hear, "Hey! Life happens!" I find this train of thinking highly suspect. For me, "Life happens" is right up there with the big bang theory. It's just hard for me to wrap my mind around the concept that something as sophisticated as the human body and the world we all inhabit just happened—poof!—or just *evolved*. I *cannot* put this together.

I don't know of one thing that manifests instantly from nothing. Every living thing is a majorly complex design. It had to have a Master Architect, Designer, Creator, Manufacturer—that would be God. To believe otherwise flies in the face of common sense and the progression we see unfolding around us every day.

Though God created the master plan, we have a lot to do with how life goes, whether we want to own our contribution to it or not. The truths we run away from have a way of swallowing us up, kinda like Jonah in the belly of the big fish. Don'tcha just love that story? Jonah, like all of humankind, had choices, and his choices had consequences. (If you're scratching your head about now, you can read the story in the Manufacturer's Guide—the Bible—in the book of Jonah and see what happens when someone makes the wrong choice.)

Because the Divine Architect has wired you with this amazing thing called *choice*, whether you like it or not, life waits for you to guide it. Left to their own devices, most things run amuck. In everything from a garden to a child, we've seen the effects of neglect and allowing things to "find their own way." A car speeding down a road will crash if you just let it go, but when you take it firmly by the wheel, it will take you to your desired destination. Even in this world of high technology, every computer awaits commands. It has to be programmed to give you what you want. No house is built without a blueprint. Each part awaits the hands of a gifted workman to put it together.

Such is life. You will get out of it what you put in. Some people invest little or nothing at all and then get upset as they watch others "living large." In urbanese we call these people *haters*. What haters don't seem to get is that those they envy paid a price to be where they are and acquire what they have.

Everyone in life selects his or her path. *Mentors* and *life coaches* have become major buzzwords as people try to solve the mystery of how to make life work for them through the guidance and experience of others. But at the end of the day, how you put your life together and run it will be up to you—regardless of surrounding input.

Some have said the best flattery a person can receive from someone is to be imitated. I heard the actor Will Smith say during an interview that he was successful because he studied the movements of other successful people and modeled himself after them. I'm sure that *part* of his success is due to imitation of others' decisions, but I think the greater part of his success lay in the organic, intangible things he brought to the table and learned to use to the benefit of others as well as himself.

The problem with imitations is they will never be as great as the original, therefore, no matter whom you imitate, you must be able to deal with your life as a separate and unique entity. What works for one might not necessarily work for the other. We are all soooo different. Yet God created us to function a certain basic way with variations according to the models we are.

Are there any hard-and-fast rules? Foundational truths are infallible. But other aspects of building the life you want will have to be adjusted to what you can handle and the effort you are willing to exert. Again, what works for one may not work for another, but the one irrefutable truth is that *what you make of your life is entirely up to you.*

I have designed this manual to help you get your life together and keep it together; to clarify some issues, help you get focused, assist you in prioritizing your goals and desires, and empower you to get the life you want and the love you need.

We will take a look at the aspects essential to making life work— what it takes to maintain the life you've selected and keep it on course. We will also examine some of the accessories you will need to customize your life to your personal specifications—in other words, make it work for you. You will always want to make additions and adjustments and decorate. You will find that different seasons of your life will cause you to want to tear down and overhaul some sections.

This is where the Master Architect's Blueprint comes in handy. Keep in mind that whether you believe in the Creator or not, His creation will still function according to His design—this is called *universal law.* It needs no acknowledgment from the creation; it generates its own power. I highly recommend to anyone attempting to put the pieces of his or her life together in a beneficial manner that he or she read the Blueprint.

Wherever you are in the project of your life, this user's manual will offer you sound principles to give you great results—results that are not only helpful but sustainable. No temporary fixes here! We are in this together for the long haul, beyond initial construction. Your life should last even after you've "moved out of the building," so to speak. That is what we call *leaving a legacy*—an impression in the lives of all you touch.

So as you study this manual, take notes, discuss with a friend, ponder, and journal—take your time, be honest with yourself, and make adjustments where necessary. Whatever you do, don't proceed without clear instructions and adherence to the guidelines of the Master Architect.

My friend, the only way a life gets transformed is when a person begins a new way of thinking, one that embraces a purposeful and strategic approach to getting the outcome he or she desires. The first thing you must do when addressing your life is to understand that it doesn't just happen.

On that note, let's take a look at this most intricate thing called life and figure out how to *work it* instead of allowing it to *work you*!

How to Make
L fe Work

Foundation:
The Four
Cornerstones

❋ You

❋ God

❋ Purpose

❋ Others

It's All in the Foundation

You can build a pretty building, but it will be only as good as its foundation. If the foundation is unstable or uneven, after a while the walls will begin to shift, causing unsightly cracks and making the house unsafe. Left untended, the cracked foundation will eventually crumble to pieces. Such is life.

And trust me, the life you build is the life you will live in. Others may come and go, but you will be stuck with what you construct. You can dress it up, but if it's not well put together under all of that dressing, eventually the outside will reflect the inside chaos. Then you will have a fine mess that you can no longer prop up for the world to see.

What is your life built upon? Your answer will give you many clues as to why life may or may not be working for you. Whether it be your appearance, material acquisitions, career achievements, or even who you know—these are all temporary things that cannot offer a sustainable platform for your life to stand upon.

Understand, right away, that your life doesn't have to look like anyone else's life. Why? Because it is uniquely and amazingly yours! Between you and the Master Architect, you will choose how to decorate and finish your life.

Certain choices you make will determine what your life will look like. Depending on how much work you apply to your choices, you will have a stable or precarious existence. Here, at the foundation, is not the place to play cheap. You will get as much out of your life as you put into it; therefore, build carefully and generously and don't cut corners.

As we examine the foundational structure of your life, we will make sure you have everything you need to secure it for the long haul: we will look at the four cornerstones of your foundation and make sure you're building with solid materials, and we will consider how to maintain the life you've constructed and keep it healthy and whole.

Are you ready to make a statement? To claim your space and leave your mark on life? Know, going in, that life is like a house: you will never be finished making it what you want it to be; there will always be room for improvement. It takes a lifetime to master and fine-tune. However, keeping it free of structural damage is up to you more than you know.

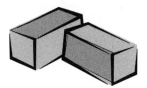

You

This is the only time I will use the phrase "It is all about you!"— because in this instance, it is. You are the most important part in the building of your life. Nothing good, bad, great, or indifferent will happen without your involvement and participation. Look at it this way: you need four corners of a foundation for a house (or life) to stand up straight and withstand whatever storms come its way. Without you, the house would lack sufficient support and cave in.

The Master Architect has created you with two very important features that should help in your pursuit of a well-built life: responsibility and authority. He fully realizes that you cannot exercise responsibility without authority. The most important things you must do when putting your life together are to (1) take responsibility for you—because at the end of the day, you are the only person who will be able to answer for your life, and (2) use your authority to make decisions wisely. Trying to make decisions without the authority to do so creates anarchy.

So now that this has been settled, get ready to look at you.

Who Are You?

You Are Unique

So, what about you? Well, just as no two snowflakes are created alike, each possessing its own pattern, you are an original. Though someone might bear a close resemblance to you, he or she will never be quite like you.

You Are Expensive

Not only are you unique—you are an extremely expensive cornerstone. The Master Architect paid dearly for you. Exchanging the life of His only Son for your life was the greatest sacrifice ever made, and yet He did it gladly to acquire you. Like the *Mona Lisa* at the Louvre, you as His child would be a star attraction should He choose to put lives on display. People are His most prized and costly possession in the whole elaborate design of life.

You Have the Power to Affect Other People

Not only are you priceless—you were created with the amazing capacity to affect others' lives in profound ways—perhaps to change the course of history by one thing you say, don't say, do, or don't do! Amazing! Intricate, complex, sophisticated—you cannot be duplicated. Your particular role in the Architect's plan is one only you can fulfill.

You Are Necessary

Not only are you an original—you are very necessary in the scheme of the Master Architect's design. Life cannot work without you. Your presence and participation are connected to the success not only of your life, but also of other people's lives. This is the ripple effect—call it "six degrees of separation," but everybody somehow affects everyone else everywhere at some point in time. Think about it: something as simple as a sneeze can set off an epidemic!

Your particular role in the Architect's plan is one only you can fulfill.

As one life connects to another, we are all tied together in ways that cannot be explained or fully understood. The effects of one man or woman's decisions can impact the entire world and change the way we all live on any given day.

You Have a Special Outer Casing

You have been created with an outer casing that identifies you. How you decorate that casing will define you even more to others. While man looks on the outer appearance, it is important for you to remember that the Master Architect will always be far more concerned with what is going on with your internal makeup (1 Sam. 16:7). Yes, He will be looking at your heart.

You Have a Heart

Your heart is at the center of you and is a key part, along with your mind and your soul, of what makes you tick. Your heart is so powerful, it influences the mind and soul.

Your heart has the capacity to wreak havoc on your system—or stop you altogether. This inner mechanism must be kept clean from life-threatening debris at all times. (See the *How to Make Love Work* manual for more info on this.)

The way you are wired becomes evident when we look at the inner chambers of the heart. What you harbor there will manifest itself outwardly in your words and actions. This is why it is important not to harbor unhealthy thoughts and attitudes in this section of your being: they can pervert sound judgment, entice you to make bad choices, and repel the very things you want to attract to your life.

More on this later—suffice it to say for now that you are more powerful than you know. The power you have to make life work for you or against you is unspeakable. The effect you have on the lives of others is deeper than you realize. For this very reason, you should take care and pay attention to the details and use your time well as you build a house—or a life that works. After all, tomorrow is not promised to anyone. You may not get the chance to remove what you put in place!

It's All on You

As mentioned before, the responsibility for how your life turns out rests on you. You are the only thing in the scheme of life that you can control; therefore, you have everything to do with how your life runs its course. You can never blame anyone else for the way you live. Will situations ever careen out of your control? Of course. In those moments, the way you respond will affect how quickly you rebound from the unexpected and seemingly unmanageable aspects of life.

You will have an amazing tool at your disposal—which I mentioned earlier—that has been built into the life of every single person on the face of the earth. It is called *choice*. The Master Architect created you with free will—you are a free agent. You can choose to answer to Him and line up with His design, or you can do your own thing.

Warning: doing your own thing might be dangerous to your health on many levels. I have found that those who do not adhere to the Master Architect's Blueprint find themselves broken, or at least deeply scarred, by the consequences of their freewheeling choices. Healthy boundaries must be set in order for every life to work as it should.

Why? Because life needs order to function at its best. Chaos is not conducive to living a good life. Exactly how much control do you have? More than you think. It is all in how you approach building your life coupled with how you feel about you. You will be able to do only what you believe you can. This is why it is important to know yourself, like yourself, love yourself, be in tune with yourself. Know what you have to offer, what you bring to the world.

Examine the Different Aspects of You

So look at yourself. Get to know you. What makes you tick? What gives you a charge? What depletes your energy and sucks the life right out of you? What feeds you? What makes you operate at your best? Find out how you are wired. Here are some aspects to consider while you are sizing yourself up:

- Are you a night person or a day person?
- Do you function best in a crowd or in isolation?
- What are your strengths and weaknesses?
- What is your temperament?
- Are you an extrovert or introvert?
- Are you a natural-born leader or a valuable team player?
- Are you detail oriented or someone who keeps the big picture in view?

There are no wrong answers here! The more you know yourself, the more you will understand where you fit in life and how to be most effective and victorious. You will also know what works against your moving forward with life in a productive manner. In other words, you will know what *works* for you.

What Will You Do with Yourself?

You get to choose if you will be a gift to the world or a liability. You get to channel all of your energy and focus toward attitudes and beliefs that can have enormously positive, lasting effects in your immediate sphere of influence and perhaps beyond. This is exciting! No need for comparison, for feeling "lesser than" or "greater than." All parts are needed in the big picture of life. Collectively we all make life happen as a whole, though each individual has a personal contribution to make to the big picture.

The bottom line is you are just one part of something much larger than you, yet you are necessary to complete the picture of what life should look like. The Master Architect's Blueprint (that would be the Bible) says it best:

> The body has many different parts, not just one part. If the foot says, "I am not a part of the body because I am not a hand," that does not make it any less a part of the body. And if the ear says, "I am not part of the body because I am only an ear and not an eye," would that make it any less a part of the body? Suppose the whole body were an eye—then how would you hear? Or if your whole body were just one big ear, how could you smell anything?
>
> …God made our bodies with many parts, and he has put each part just where he wants it. What a strange thing a body would be if it had only one part! Yes, there are many parts, but only one body. The eye can never say to the hand, "I don't need you." The head can't say to the feet, "I don't need you."
>
> In fact, some of the parts that seem weakest and least important are really the most necessary. (1 Corinthians 12:14–22)

Wow! So even though you are you, there is a connection between you and the world at large! You have a major part to play in the scenario of life. How instrumental you are in the world's being a better place is entirely up to you.

Since you will be a foundational stone in this thing called life, how you place yourself in relation to the other three cornerstones of the foundation is vitally important. We'll look at this next.

CONSTRUCTION TIP
There can be only one you, unique and crafted to do what only you can do. Any duplicates or counterfeits will fall apart under pressure.

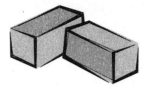

God

S ome would ask why the God Cornerstone of the foundation is mentioned *after* the You Cornerstone. The God Cornerstone is actually the primary stone needed in life, yet you have to choose to use it. It is crucial for you to understand, while attempting to build a secure "house," that your life does "not consist in the abundance of [your] possessions" (Luke 12:15 NIV). Though you acquire much, if your connection to God is not rich, you can still live a bankrupt life.

Whether you choose to acknowledge and utilize the God Cornerstone or not, His initial design for life is universal law. There's really no way of getting around Him. He is the center of all things because He created all things. Some use portions of His Blueprint without acknowledging Him and still reap the fruit of His wisdom. *Warning:* this is not recommended, as this is a short-term "fix" rather than a long-term solution for an eternal existence.

Life as you know it does not end when physical death occurs. Actually it is just beginning! Every person will have to address the issue of eternal life at some point; full safety and security can be secured only by anchoring yourself in direct alignment with the God Cornerstone. That is, you need God and His instructions as your foundation in order to exist with sustained victory. Everything else is like slapping a Band-aid on a badly bleeding wound. You'll find yourself wondering why it slips off when life gets wet. Nothing else lasts.

As I mentioned earlier, God made provision for you to enjoy eternal life with Him through His Son, Jesus. Jesus is the official beginning and end of life as we know it and beyond. "In him we live and move and have our being" (Acts 17:28 NIV). "Apart from [Him] you can do nothing" (John 15:5 NIV). Don't believe the hype of those who proclaim that you are God, the head of your own destiny. Not true! And it only takes one day of your life's being totally out of control—no matter how much good you project—to find that out.

Who would want all that responsibility anyway? There is great comfort in knowing that someone greater has your back and your best interest at heart *and* can do something about the impossible places you sometimes find yourself in. Say to yourself as many times as you need to in order to set yourself free: "He is God; I am not!" This simple truth is short and sweet but huge in the scheme of life.

The God Cornerstone is extraordinarily strong, as it is made up of three separate yet equally strong components. The first is the Father component. By the way, use of the term *Father* does not imply that God is male. This is a positional reference to His function as Provider, Protector, and Giver of Life. "God is spirit" (John 4:24 NIV), which encompasses all genders and races. In Him there is no male or female, slave or free, Greek or Jew (Gal. 3:28). He is the Giver, Sustainer, and empowering Force of life. It is impossible to construct and maintain a life of any great quality without this component in your foundation cornerstone.

Second, the Jesus component is put in place not only for you to have eternal security but also life here on Earth. And not just any ole life—He wants you to have it "abundantly" (John 10:10 NASB).

Last but not least, the Holy Spirit is the component that gives instruction, interprets the will of the Father, and reveals the heart and inner workings of the Father and the Son. This component is the stabilizing part of the God Cornerstone if we embrace it and utilize it. It generates power to all who need to be sustained or fueled for the journey of life.

Who *Is* God, Anyway?

Great question! Another one is: why can't we *be* Him even though He empowers us to be *like* Him? Well, when Moses was talking with God and receiving His command to take His people out of Egypt, he said: "If I go to the people and tell them, 'The God of your ancestors has sent me to you,' they won't believe me. They will ask, 'Which God are you talking about? What is his name?' Then what shall I tell them?" God answered, "Just tell them, 'I AM has sent me to you'" (Exod. 3:13–14).

Straight to the point. Whatever it is you need, God says, I AM that. No human being can say that. You and I can be a few things one at a time, but He is *all* things all the time: Lord of the Universe, Healer, Deliverer, Savior, Mighty Counselor, all-knowing, all-powerful—whew! No one else can fill His shoes.

This is why He is the Master Architect, the original Designer. And yet He is gracious enough to give us portions of Himself that empower us to be wise, creative, resourceful, and resilient. Wow! That is powerful. God, the chief cornerstone of your life's foundation, is phenomenal.

Still, many of us long for even more power than what God has given us. Before you ask for more, consider this: are you actually using the power you already have to full capacity? God is interesting because even though He is almighty, He wants to work through us, and with us. It is this divine connection and partnership that empowers us to build the lives we want to live and sustain the quality of life we so deeply desire. That is who God is.

What Does God Bring to the Table?

Besides the life of His Son, what does God offer us to enable us to live the lives we want both naturally and spiritually? Good question.

You see, God understands how you are constructed better than you do! He understands that you are a spirit that has a soul that lives in a body. Therefore He addresses every part of you. The Blueprint tells us, "What came first was the natural body, then the spiritual body comes later" (1 Cor. 15:46). Man was a natural and physical entity before God breathed into him, imparting His own spirit into the soul of man, making him a spiritual being as well.

It is important for you to know that God is passionately interested in every aspect of your life: from what you wear and eat to how you feel to where you will spend eternity. He wants to be involved with your entire being—heart, soul, mind, and body. He wants to touch you physically, spiritually, and emotionally. He has a plan and guidelines for all of these aspects and more.

The sacrifice of His Son, Jesus, is His way of dealing with your address after you leave your earthly building (your natural body). Through relationship with Jesus you are granted access to a right or reconciled relationship with God (through forgiveness of your sin and imperfections) and a place called heaven.

Some have argued against heaven's existence as a physical place, yet it is clearly described that way in the Master Architect's Blueprint (Mark 16:19, 2 Cor. 5:1). It is far more substantial than a state of mind or a sort of emotional well-being. And trust me, if what we experience on Earth is as good as it gets, a lot of people would have to wonder why we should continue if we have nothing better to anticipate. Indeed, God knows we all look forward to a greater glory than what we experience on Earth—a true utopia where God will be present and all will be in divine order—life at its ultimate best.

God is passionately interested in every aspect of your life.

Though God is interested in our physical health (we will delve into this further later), He informs us that we do "not live by bread alone, but by every word that proceeds from the mouth of God" (Matt. 4:4 NKJV). His Word and instructions actually feed us. His Word becomes not only the compass for our lives but our sustenance, our vitamins, the thing that empowers us to keep going even when life is not working the way we want it to.

God's promises fuel us. They give us the impetus to stay on track and keep moving forward in spite of what our eyes see. There are tens of thousands of promises in the Bible. A promise from someone can keep you going even when the way looks uncertain.

If your best friend told you she would meet you at a specific restaurant on a given day at a specific time, you would not call her every five minutes to make sure she was still coming. You would go on faith that she would be true to her word. Well, God is the "friend who sticks closer" than any other (Prov. 18:24 NIV). What He says, He will do, because He cannot and will not lie. He is true to His promises (Num. 23:19). He knows that "hope deferred [repeated disappointment] makes the heart sick, but a longing fulfilled is a tree of life" (Prov. 13:12 NIV). He will not let us down because He is all about giving life!

The only way to know and be able to believe these promises is to nurture your relationship with God—get to know Him, how His mind works. Understanding what moves the hand and heart of God is crucial to your relationship. Spend time with Him. Read His Word. Talking with and listening to Him deepens your relationship as you learn more and more about Him and His ways...and how much He loves you!

As your relationship grows, God's ways and nature become contagious. Your mind begins to change and your life is transformed into the life you've been praying for (Rom. 12:2).

Nothing changes without relationship—but more on that later. Suffice it to say for now that the God Cornerstone of your foundation is crucial to a life well lived. Without this corner, a major part of your life will be missing. Though you might not be able to say exactly what it is, the void will be apparent, painfully so, to you and those around you. Your foundation will not be stable enough to support anything you build on it long term.

No achievements, acquisitions, or people can replace God in the building of a life that works. But when God is present, you've got the foundation for building a solid life that will stand the test of time.

Line up the God Cornerstone for perfect alignment with the You Cornerstone.

CONSTRUCTION TIP
There is only one God. He is the only aspect of the life you are building that is not manufactured. He is the beginning and end of life, because He is the source of it. You can't get around Him because He is larger than life!

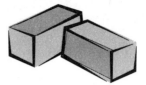

Purpose

Purpose ignites living, giving life meaning and power. Contrary to popular belief, no one on our planet is here by accident. If your parents didn't "plan" you, God still had you in mind long before you became a reality. He knew you before you were born (Ps. 139:13, 15–16; Rom. 8:29), and your purpose was already in place, waiting for you to show up and claim it.

Deep in every human being's heart is the question, *What on earth am I here for?* The Divine Architect and Creator has designed us all to desire to do more than just stand around sucking up air. We were created to make a contribution to the world at large and to impact the kingdom of God. Trust me—"The earth is the LORD's, and all its fullness, the world and those who dwell therein"—whether folks behave as if it is or not (Ps. 24:1 NKJV).

Therefore, embrace your purpose and fulfill your part in this vast universe. This cornerstone of your foundation gives you the significance that every person on the face of the earth craves.

God's Plans and Purpose Defined

You were deliberately placed where you can be a part of something that is so much bigger than you, it is phenomenal even to consider. Let's look at a few aspects of your purpose.

He Created You to Worship

First, you were created to be a worshipper, to walk in fellowship with the God of the universe (John 4:23). He desires a relationship with you. He is passionate about you and wants the door of communication between you and Himself to be a much-used entryway. This is huge: God considers you soooo significant, *He craves to be near you.* He derives joy from associating with you. You bless His heart when you draw near and seek Him.

Worship encompasses everything you do, from waking and praising Him in the morning, to helping a stranger, to choosing to obey Him when your flesh craves something else.

"Worship mode" is the greatest level your life can function on. Worship is complete submission to and cooperation with God, and it is your "reasonable" act of gratitude for all He has done and supplied for you (Rom. 12:1 NKJV). This should be a permanent and unending pursuit in your life, to live in worship of God. Enacting this part of your purpose keeps you in prime condition to function in all areas—to build a life that has meaning and depth.

He Created You to Bear Spiritual Fruit

Next, He wants you to be fruitful in your life—yes, productive. This is a reflection of His creative nature. Everything God creates bears fruit, and He wants you to be the same.

God wants you to reflect His personality and attributes to the world so that others can see His goodness working through you and be attracted to Him (Matt. 5:16). This is called *bearing spiritual fruit*.

Your behavior and attitudes start a chain reaction: You interact with God. You see His goodness. His goodness changes you. Others notice those changes, which become contagious. Good fruit is inviting to everyone! It smells sweet. It looks appealing. It is desirable for tasting. People want a good thing. So if you look, smell, and are like God, not only will people desire a relationship with you, they will also want to know more about the One who made you the way you are.

After seeing Him for themselves, they won't need you to convince them of His goodness. You will be the conduit of a divine connection that blesses everyone! That is the best spiritual fruit you can produce. That is your purpose.

He Created You to Make Disciples

Being "fruitful" is part of Jesus' last command in the Gospels: "Go and make disciples of all the nations" (Matt. 28:19). Again, if you are producing good fruit, people will want whatever you have enabling you to produce that good fruit. This allows you to "make disciples"—add believers to the kingdom of God—as you share your faith and relationship with the One who made you fruitful.

He Created You to Subdue Evil

Evil unravels the very fabric of the world. One wrong action can cause a ripple effect that touches the lives of countless people. Consider this: one man tried to board a plane with an explosive in his shoe. Now every person on the planet who flies commercially must remove his or her shoes and endure intense scrutiny before boarding a plane.

It is a fact of life that the majority rules. It is important to be an influence for bringing people to the kingdom of God, so that light will overtake the darkness in all areas of life. We are called to raise a standard that encourages light and life not just for ourselves, but for the world.

He Created You to Engage in Spiritual Warfare

What you cannot accomplish in conversation and example, be assured you can accomplish in prayer and spiritual warfare. The greatest battles over evil have been won by those who understood the power of prayer and intercession (prayer for others). As I've pointed out, "We are not fighting against people made of flesh and blood, but against the evil rulers and authorities of the unseen world, against those mighty powers of darkness who rule this world, and against wicked spirits in the heavenly realms" (Eph. 6:12). Because of this, we do not strike out at those who stand before us but rather look past them to the real source of trouble and deal with it in the Spirit.

We deal with the invisible by using prayer as a weapon to do battle against the things we cannot control in the natural realm. By praying and confessing the Word of God and what He says about our particular circumstance, we replace the lies that come from the enemy of our souls with the truth. Submitting to God and resisting the mind-sets and the temptations the enemy presents to us also help us to be overcomers.

He Created You to Walk in Confidence and Authority

We do this through prayer, example, and encouragement of others. We are to have life; life is not to have us. As a matter of fact, Jesus said that the thief (the evil one) came to steal, kill, and destroy our lives, but Jesus came so we could enjoy life "in all its fullness" (John 10:10).

This means we follow the design of the Master Architect and come to the full stature of who He designed us to be, that is, we grow and mature spiritually. Because of who and whose we are, we are not upset by circumstances. We know our spiritual rights and we stand firm in them.

What does this mean in practical terms? We should be agents of

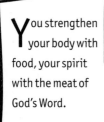
You strengthen your body with food, your spirit with the meat of God's Word.

change. When we enter a room, we should bring peace where chaos once ruled. When we converse with nonbelievers, we aren't shy about what we believe. When we face hardship, we don't give in to despair.

Why? Because the very Spirit of God abides inside of us, and the Spirit is powerful and life-changing. This is why we should choose to walk purposefully, undistracted by things that feed the flesh but starve our spirits and rob us of power. You strengthen your body with food, your spirit with the meat of God's Word.

He Created You to Bear Natural Fruit

Then of course there is the natural—physical, relational, and professional—fruit.

Physical fruit. For women, there is most obviously the fruit of the womb: children you can raise and give as a gift to the world. Motherhood will show you more about how God feels about you than anything else can. As you try, with all that is within you, to show your children the right way, to care for and nurture them, even through the thankless times and the times they go astray, you love them. They are an extension of you, a reflection of you. You were there from the beginning. You see their potential. And even when they don't live up to it, you are grieved but you love them anyway—kinda like God.

Relational fruit. Beyond what you produce from your body, there is the fruit of your relationships—what you add to the life of others. This is all about how you increase love, joy, peace, patience, kindness, goodness, faithfulness, gentleness, and discipline, not only in your life but also in the lives of those around you (Gal. 5:22–23).

Let me give you an example. I attended the funeral of a wonderful man. People told countless stories of the joy he had given them through service, compassion, encouragement, a great sense of humor, and even a mischievous streak. But more than this, he inspired all in attendance to be better people because of his example.

How about you—what would you like to inspire in others? What great legacy will you leave behind? Better yet, what do you want others to say about you? What would you have to do to get them to say those things? It's good food for thought.

Take stock of your relationships. Strong, enduring friendships say a lot about you as a person. A revolving door of acquaintances and shipwrecked relationships says something too. If we are to experience good fruit in our relationships, we will have to be cognizant of how we nurture relationships that are precious to us.

Of course, not all relationships are on the same level. There are what I call *outer-court acquaintances, inner-court friends,* and then your *holy of holies inner circle.* Though each one may fill a different area of need or operate at a different level of closeness, everyone in your life deserves respect and honor from you. Treat each one as a special gift from God.

We cannot operate or thrive apart from others. We were wired to be relational. Our relationships strengthen us to stand when we grow weary and empower us to keep moving when we would rather quit and roll over. Your relationships will be one of the greatest forms of fruit you bear. Strong, God-honoring relationships are part of your Purpose Cornerstone in the foundation of a well-built life. These relationships will add support as needed to your life and, in some instances, keep you from crumbling.

Professional fruit. By definition, a profession can be the words of your mouth or what you do. Both reveal important parts of who you are. The work of your hands is the expression of the passion you harbor in your heart.

No matter what role you play professionally, you are absolutely necessary. So be productive wherever you are. There really are no

menial tasks, only those who don't see the value and meaning associated with each area of work. Each profession not only carries honor
but is vital to making life work for everyone. The Blueprint tells us,
"We are God's masterpiece. He has created us anew in Christ Jesus,
so that we can do the good things he planned for us long ago" (Eph.
2:10). More on this later, but again, this is part of your purpose: to do
"good things" that benefit those around you.

You can know the character of a person by his or her fruit (Matt.
7:16). Some fruit looks good until you squeeze it—then you find out
that it is bruised or rotten. When life puts the squeeze on you, whatever is in you is sure to come to light. People will know you by your
"fruit" as well.

✣

THE CORRECT FOUNDATION is everything to a house that stands
straight and lasts long. Avoid careless placement. Align the Purpose
Cornerstone in exact alignment with the You and God Cornerstones.
You now have three solid corners of a firm foundation. We'll look at
the fourth next.

CONSTRUCTION TIP
No matter what you add to your foundation, if the Purpose
Cornerstone is missing, life will collapse from the buildup
of discontent and hopelessness.

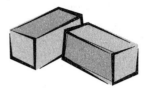

Others

This is the final aspect of your all-important foundation. It's been said that no man is an island, and this is true. We are wired to connect with others, to encourage, uplift, support, provoke one another to good works, and counsel one another along what can be, at times, an arduous journey.

Because you were created to connect with others, your relationships can make or break your life. The right associations can empower you to make good choices that cause you to flourish; the wrong associations can topple your entire "house"!

Since others come into our lives in different shapes and sizes and serve different purposes, let's look at them separately. Four areas of relationship solidify this cornerstone and fortify you to stand no matter what elements or circumstances you confront in life: your relationships with God, with yourself, with your family, friends, coworkers, and associates, and with your spouse. All of these people make up the core that is central to how you function and interact with the rest of the world at large—i.e., how well your life works.

Your Relationship with God

You can't get far in life without confronting the questions of your humanity, your insufficiency to live a sinless life, your purpose for existence on this earth, and the phenomenal question of life after death—whether it exists and what that means for you. Some of this will remain a mystery until the end of time, when we finally see God face-to-face. In the meantime, He is the only One who can give you solid answers concerning all of those issues. People who do not know their God cannot know themselves. He is the Revealer of our identity and all that we harbor in our hearts.

Identity

If you don't embrace your God-given identity (or purpose), you are a sojourner wandering in the land without direction. Directionless people are hopeless people. Without this divine connection, life is full of questions and uncertainties: *Who am I? What is my reason for being here? Do I really matter?*

Without a sense of the significance that only God can give, you run the risk of becoming a great pretender with an inflated air of self-importance that affects all the other relationships that lend support in life.

Joy

Your relationship with God is crucial, not only because He solidifies your identity, but because He is the One who gives you true joy. He gives you a joy that the world can't take away—a joy that empowers you.

Peace

Along with joy He gives you a peace that defies understanding. Having peace with God comes from doing the right thing, thereby being in right standing with Him. When you are right with God, you don't need validation from anyone else to make you feel right about yourself or your decisions. This is the ultimate peace.

> If you don't embrace your God-given identity (or purpose), you are a sojourner wandering in the land without direction.

You will be able to keep your cool when everyone around you is losing theirs—and keeping your cool is important in order for life to work well. Being volatile, irrational, and out of control can seriously impede your progress, if not grind your life to a screeching halt.

Strength

Last but not least, your relationship with God provides strength. Your interaction with Him and your knowledge that He is in your corner empowers you. Those "who know their God shall be strong, and carry out great exploits" (Dan. 13:22 NKJV).

Knowing God is imperative to overcoming. Don't believe the hype: you can go only so far in your own strength before you need the auxiliary power that comes from relationship with the Master Architect. Life is not truly life without Him—here in the present and certainly not in eternity!

Your Relationship with Yourself

Only in having a relationship with God can you have fruitful relationships with yourself and with others. You cannot love what you don't know, whether we are talking about God, yourself, or others. Being able to truthfully assess yourself in light of what God has said about you helps you know your strengths and weaknesses and what you have to offer to the world. Knowing the specifics of your spiritual gifts puts a smile on your face, a pep in your step, and generosity in your heart.

The commandment to "love the Lord your God with all your heart, and with all your soul, with all your mind, and with all your strength" is critical, but so is the commandment that follows: "You shall love your neighbor as yourself" (Mark 12:30–31 ESV). For you to love your neighbor as yourself, this verse says, you must first love you! Not in a self-involved, narcissistic way, but in a way that shows you accept who you are and the way God created you. You are all right with the world (not afraid of it or hostile toward it in general) and at peace with yourself. You like the skin you are in and have a healthy understanding of your own value. A friend once told me, "If I met myself walking down the street, I would want to be my friend." What an awesome concept—to have such a healthy appreciation of yourself that you could say such a thing!

If you don't know or love yourself, you will be much more prone to criticize others. Others will feel your discomfort with yourself, and they will avoid you. They might not even know what is wrong, but most people instinctively avoid unhappy campers. You need to know that you are "fearfully and wonderfully made" (Ps. 139:14 NIV). This means that God created you as you are and thought you were amazing indeed! He admires all of His handiwork and calls it good, and that includes you.

Make a decision to celebrate your strengths and work on your weaknesses. Stop beating yourself up and turn your attention outward toward others. As you love and bless others, you will begin to feel loved and blessed yourself!

Amazing and fruitful relationships with others begin with your relationship with yourself. If you know and love yourself, you will have no problem loving others. To accept yourself is to be able to celebrate others. People always want to be around someone who encourages and celebrates them! Don't you?

Let's face it: everyone struggles with so many issues in life, everyone is looking for a happy distraction. You can be that distraction—depending on what you see when you stand in front of the mirror. I'm not talking about the full-length mirror, although body image can affect how you feel about yourself. I'm talking about the internal person, who you really are: the one most people don't get a chance to see but probably should. The authentic you. The person God created you to be!

Knowing yourself, being honest about what you need to fix, tighten up, or overhaul—let's be honest; we all have some rough areas that need sanding—as well as appreciating the attractive features of who you are prepares you to be a major contributor to all you encounter. Loving yourself releases you to reach out to others in healing ways—something they will appreciate and learn to do for others as well.

Everyone you touch should be the better for it: coworkers, neighbors (do you even know them?), those you encounter on a daily basis. I think of a woman named Tabitha who was so loving and caring that when she died, the women gathered to mourn her death and rehearse her good deeds (Acts 9:36). Her passing so grieved the women that when the apostle Peter arrived, he was moved to raise her back to life!

Now that's what I'm talking about: so deeply affecting the lives of others that the good things you do live on even after you are gone. Talk about a life that works! In a sense, what you do for others will bring you back to life.

Family

Family is not an optional part of your Others Cornerstone. You don't get to choose who these people are. Though sometimes family members are dysfunctional, for the most part, no one can do without these very significant people. Your family anchors you. You can allow members to shape you or not—that is your choice.

Family is also your first interaction with community, how different people challenge and cooperate with one another. This is where you learn to give honor to all others. Here is where you learn what your strengths and weaknesses are, what you need from other people, and what you have to give. Yes, your home is a mini-kingdom!

Let's look first at the most influential aspects of your Others Cornerstone: your parents.

Parents

We've heard the apple doesn't fall far from the tree, implying that you will be just like your mother or father, yet it is important to know that no one has to be stuck in modes of behavior passed down or modeled by a parent. Each day we all get to choose life or death, blessing or curses, on an individual basis (Josh. 24:15). You have the power to choose life—and abundant life at that.

In the Master Architect's Blueprint, God states:

> Suppose that a sinful son, in turn, has a son who sees his father's wickedness but decides against that kind of life. Suppose this son refuses to worship idols on the mountains, does not commit adultery, is fair to debtors and does not rob them. And suppose this son feeds the hungry, provides clothes for the needy, helps the poor, does not lend money at interest, and obeys all my regulations and laws. Such a person will not die…he will surely live. (Ezekiel 18:14–17)

No one ever has to feel stuck because of the people he or she came from. You are not doomed to fall into patterns of behavior you neither like nor respect in your parents (or anyone else, for that matter). You never have to hear the words "You are just like your mother [or father]!" if you don't want to. It is your choice to take the deck you've been dealt and reshuffle the cards any way you please.

Sometimes parents come as a couple, sometimes they don't. Of course, the Creator's preference is that you have two parents, but you can enjoy an excellent life with just one, if that one is solid and God-honoring. Coupled with the God Cornerstone, aligned with the Purpose and You Cornerstones, your Others foundation Cornerstone can be just as secure as those of people with two parents.

Sometimes external additions are added to the family unit (step-parents) who also strengthen the Others Cornerstone. I am privileged to have two extraordinary fathers. Mr. Hammond is my natural father. Mr. McKinney married my mother, who is amazing in her own right, when I was seven and became an amazing addition to my life. He adopted me and treated me as his own. He also graciously shared me when I was reunited with my father in high school. I have continued to be surrounded by the love of my two fathers. Together they made mutual decisions about my life and presented them as a united front. I never saw an opening to play two parts against the middle. Through teamwork, they guided me on the major decisions of my life. I felt championed and bolstered to do my best without the distraction of division on their parts.

Parents are necessary for foundational security. They give you direction and inspire, encourage, and equip you to stand on your own as a responsible and considerate member of the community.

Parents should prepare you for the world at large. They become your guideposts, showing you the right ways to go and giving you all relevant information for a successful life. They are also responsible for your maintenance until you are capable of maintaining yourself.

Parents (good ones, that is) are valuable on countless levels, some evident (provision, security, love, instruction), some almost subliminal. Parents are your first encounter with authority. As you learn the importance of yielding to leadership at home, you will better understand the significance and importance of submission when you venture out into the world. Even Jesus "learned obedience from the things he suffered" (Heb. 5:8). If you do not master obedience at home, you will encounter difficulty in every other area of life—trust me on this.

Meanwhile, the God Cornerstone supplies you with everything you need, as the apostle James points out: "His divine power has given to us all things that pertain to life and godliness, through the knowledge of Him who called us" (2 Pet. 1:3 NKJV). If you have these two sources of guidances—parent(s) and God—you have a great chance of building a life that works! Remember, a threefold cord is not easily broken; it is fortified to remain secure and will not fall apart under the normal wear and tear of life (Eccl. 4:9–12).

Only a few others will stand with you throughout the trials and rigors of your life. You need only a few for a strong foundation. Make sure your relationships with these key others are harmonious and unbreakable. Since the only perfect parent is God the Father, you'll have to leave room for some errors and flaws in those you love. The only person you will live with your entire life is yourself, but parents run a close second.

Siblings

You can love 'em or hate 'em, but the bottom line is you do have to live with them—and they never really go away. They can be blessings or make you wonder how you got stuck with them. Your siblings will test your strength, your grace, and your nerves; the flip side of that is in the Master Architect's Blueprint: a brother is born to help you weather hard circumstances, to be with you in time of need (Prov. 17:17).

One family I knew had twenty-six children! You'd better believe no one messed with them. Bullies were afraid they would have to take on the entire army of siblings if they started a fight with one. When I faced a bully myself, I wanted that family to adopt me! The fact is, only Jesus can stay closer than a brother or sister (Prov. 18:24), but siblings will be your greatest test of how you will interact outside the safe haven of your home.

They provide the practice ground for the real world. The health of your interaction with these significant others that make up your intimate circle will have a major effect on all of your other relationships, from friendship to marriage.

Friends

You can't pick your family, but you do get to select your friends. Choose wisely, as "bad company corrupts good character" (1 Cor. 15:33 NIV). Beware of yes-men (or yes-women)—those who tell you only what you want to hear. You need people in your life who will tell it like it is, stir your Kool-Aid, get in your face, and speak the truth in love. The "wounds of a friend can be trusted," but the kisses of an enemy are plentiful and deceitful (Prov. 27:6 NIV).

Find friends who will commit to walk with you in transparency and accountability. The world will lie to you, but your friends should not. They should love you enough to hurt you if need be.

Now this is always a sticky area, because even when someone speaks the truth in love, let's face it: sometimes the truth hurts even though it is good for us. And yet sometimes we need intense fellowship or just plain old healthy confrontation to sharpen our character, to tighten up our acts, to help us make choices that are

> You need people in your life who will tell it like it is, stir your Kool-Aid, get in your face, and speak the truth in love.

conducive to victorious living—to well-built lives. Truly, "as iron sharpens iron," so two friends should sharpen one another (Prov. 27:17 NKJV).

If you want life to work, you need to surround yourself with people who are doing what you want to do, going where you want to go, on fire for what sets your soul on fire. Add more than less to the mix of those who are ahead of you in the journey—those who have succeeded at what you are still striving to do. The bottom line is you need people in your life who spur you to be better, to do greater things (Heb. 10:24).

Your alliances should add to your life, not subtract from it. They should bring increase to you mentally, spiritually, emotionally, and physically. They should build you up, not tear you down; encourage and exhort you to grow, to dream, to flourish!

Being well connected has everything to do with your ability to be fruitful and productive or paralyzed and ineffective. Your associations will either open doors or shut them. Recently I spoke with a friend who was struggling to bring a dream to fruition. I had watched him approach many people who could help him, but they feigned interest in what he was doing only to get him to help them with what they were doing!

After a while he grew incredibly frustrated and wondered if he should give up his dream. At this point a guy invited my friend to help him part-time with a project. The guy offering the job was impressed by my friend's dream. The position he offered would provide income for my friend but still allow time and flexibility to work on his own dream.

I advised him to take it. I liked the man's enthusiasm and appreciation for my friend. I told him it was time to go where he was celebrated and not merely tolerated or used. He accepted the position. Because of this, he was in the right place at the right time to meet someone who is now assisting him with—including funding—his dream.

What had been a lengthy struggle to realize his vision was accelerated by being connected to the right person. Relationships are everything when it comes to life working for you. All the right people have to be in place and connected in the right way. Others with more experience or better connections can help you build expertly. Don't discount what the right people can contribute to your life.

Choose friends like those of the paralyzed man in Mark 2. When the man couldn't transport himself to Jesus to be healed, his friends found a way to help. They were a determined team! They literally tore a hole in the roof of the building and lowered their friend down to Jesus. A blind man in Mark 8 also had friends who made sure he got to Jesus.

You need friends in your life who won't settle into self-defeating habits with you, who will take drastic measures if need be to get you free of whatever binds you—be it a (fixable) physical problem or an emotional or spiritual one. You need friends who will intercede for you and take you to Jesus when you can't see your own way. You need friends who will promote you to good works and pull the best out of you—who won't allow you to settle to a place beneath God's calling for your life. Those are true friends.

The Ultimate Earthly Relationship

Your life partner will be your key earthly relationship. In a sense, your life partner names you and defines you. This person in particular has the power to make or break your life, to strengthen or to weaken you, to propel you into your destiny or rob you of it.

This is the person you sleep with, the person who is joined to you both physically and spiritually. The intimacy between you creates a bond more powerful than any other relationship you will have on the face of the earth. It surpasses the bond of even your parents who had a hand in creating, birthing, and nurturing you. The person with whom you have sexual union transcends any maternal or paternal ties because you literally become one with another human being. This creates a soul tie that binds you to your mate. When this covenant connection is severed, the damage is like that of an amputation. You feel the pain of missing your partner long after his or her departure. This is called *phantom pain*, and it's very real for those who've undergone an amputation either physical or emotional. (Read more about covenant in *How to Make Love Work*.)

Many wonder why the pain of losing a spouse to death or divorce is so deep and relentless. The answer is that this was no surface relationship. It penetrated beneath the skin to the soul realm. The commitment to "forever and ever, amen" is remembered by the spirit long after it has been abandoned by the intellect. You are expected to leave mother and father and cleave to your mate, becoming one with each other in an everlasting, unbreakable connection (Gen. 2:24).

Each of us spends enormous energy and time looking for his or her soul mate: the one we believe will be the cherry on top of the cake, the one who will "complete" us, our better half or other half, depending on how you look at it. This is only natural, because the first thing man received after being created by God was a kiss. God breathed into man the breath of life and man became a living soul. Exchanging breath—a kiss. To this day we all crave a lasting exchange, an endless "kiss" or connection that sets our hearts on fire and gives us life. We are designed for this soul-to-soul, heart-to-heart, mind-to-mind connection.

Your mate needs to encompass all that your friends do and more— actually, that person should be your best friend. Love that will last begins and is grounded in genuine friendship. Your mate should also, in a sense, continue the work of your parents and siblings and bring balance to your life.

If you are a woman, you were designed to be a helper to your mate. Yes, even the Architect has agreed that this part of His creation, the male, needs help. That should be empowering news to all females. You can be a Delilah, rob him of his strength, and "kill" him, or a

Deborah who helps her man fight the wars in his life. If you are married to an unbeliever, you can be an Esther and help your man do the right thing whether he acknowledges God or not. The bottom line is a woman has the power to make or break a man, so she should use her power wisely.

God holds the man responsible for loving the woman, for caring for her as if she were a part of his own body, protecting and providing for her. Women need men: they were created for men, and no matter how independent they become, they long for the tender touch of a man as well as the strength of his presence. God holds the man accountable for the woman's well-being. This should empower men to rise to the occasion and realize how important they are in women's lives.

As women, we can rest secure in the knowledge of what treasures we are in the eyes of our Creator. To think He would assign someone the task of taking care of us so tenderly suggests He considers us to be of great value.

For a more in-depth look at the intricate workings of the love mechanism, please refer to the user's manual *How to Make Love Work*. In the meantime, know that the second greatest decision in life you will make (after choosing Christ as Savior) will be that of whom you marry. This one decision will affect the rest of your life whether the marriage lasts or not.

The repercussions from a broken heart are both deep and lasting, but a love relationship that thrives can enable you to reach unbelievable heights and add the finishing touches to an incredible life. This union is so intense that when built according to the Architect's design, it empowers both partners to be more effective and fruitful than ever before.

Note: you must have a life that works well in order to have a love that works well. Why? Because whatever affects your life will affect your heart, which affects your love life. Got it? In short, the two anchor one another.

⋇

Now that we have discussed the functions of all the others who will form the fourth cornerstone of your foundation, let's list them in the order that you should honor them. God is first, of course. Then your husband (if you're married), parents, siblings, and friends. After those you can honor all additional others, such as coworkers and acquaintances.

Treasure all of the other relationships and give the honor due them. This will ensure that your priorities remain intact and this cornerstone of the foundation stays strong. Each of these important persons has a great effect on whether you make life work or not. Arrange this cornerstone of the foundation with care, in perfect alignment with the other three cornerstones.

Now you can begin to build!

CONSTRUCTION TIP
Your life will work only as well as the lives
you surround yourself with.

Pillars

- ❊ Faith
- ❊ Health
- ❊ Profession
- ❊ Finances

Pillars: The Structures That Hold Up Your Life

Some people are called "pillars of the church" or "pillars of society." These are the mainstays, the ones everyone looks to for guidance and stability. These are the guideposts, the beacons that show the way for others to follow. Many have set the standard for how others should live by forging ahead and building successful lives despite all obstacles.

As you build a life that works, you also need support structures that hold you up when everything seems to be falling apart. These are the things and people you can lean on and trust. Your life requires its own pillars in order to stand firm and last over the test of time. It's time to focus on the things that will guide your decisions for establishing a healthy life that endures all complications, distractions, and disasters.

Pillars are central to your existence—a vital ingredient in a life that works. First you have the foundation, the four cornerstones on which the whole building will stand; then you have to erect the pillars, which will hold up the walls and ceiling. Everything else in life will lean on those things that have been put in place to support the structure of your life.

Let's take an in-depth look at these pillars and how they will affect your life overall. Faith, health, profession, and finances are the four areas that most wrestle with and use as support vehicles throughout life. If these areas are working well, then life is working as a whole. When these things are in place and their stability established, most people release a sigh of relief and look at the big picture of life without concern.

Let's start with an essential pillar—that of your faith.

Faith

"For by grace you have been saved through faith" (Eph. 2:8 NASB). Grace releases us to revel in the forgiveness of God and be counted as righteous or in right standing with Him. This enables us to live by faith (Rom. 1:17) and be obedient to God (Rom. 1:5). If we build our lives around a pillar of faith, it will establish us securely for life.

What exactly is faith? It is "the confident assurance that what we hope for is going to happen. It is the evidence of things we cannot yet see" (Heb. 11:1). The English Standard Version of the Bible calls faith "the conviction of things not seen" (Heb. 11:1 ESV). What does that mean in layman's terms?

Having faith means you believe that the things you hope for in your heart and dreams will manifest themselves in tangible reality—by God's power, not yours. You know that you know that you know, so to speak, no matter what anyone says, no matter what things look like, that the vision you have is going to become real. And when it does, it will be solid evidence that you did not hope in vain.

Faith is not something you can just work up on your own—it has to be grounded in something. It works in relationship with your knowledge of God. Faith cannot rest on men's wisdom but only on God's power; the apostle Paul wrote that he used "very plain" preaching to reach the Corinthians: "I did this so that [when the preaching had a great effect] you might trust the power of God rather than human wisdom" (1 Cor. 2:4–5). Faith, the Blueprint tells us, is a result of hearing the Word of God (Rom. 10:17), because Jesus is the "author and finisher of our faith" (Heb. 12:2 NKJV).

Where Does Faith Come From?

Faith comes from knowing what God has promised you, how He works, and His long record of accomplishing great and amazing feats and annihilating adversity. I recommend having a sort of faith trophy case. This would be where you harbor the memories of the ways and times that God has come through for you in the past. In fact, this trophy case could take the form of a journal in which you record how difficult circumstances worked out for the good or even better than you imagined. This record will build confidence for when you encounter another trial—you will be able to look back and see how God worked things out for you in the past.

This practice of remembering God's deliverance is very biblical. In Psalm 103 David says, "Praise the LORD, I tell myself, and never forget the good things he does for me" (v. 2). Throughout the Old Testament, Israel's leaders called upon the people to remember all God had done for them (Deut. 5:15; 1 Chron. 16:12; Job 10:9).

You've probably learned by now that God will never allow you to sail through life minus interferences and setbacks, because this is how character gets built. (We'll cover that more later.) Much faith will be required in order for you to endure all that is ahead of you in life. Faith has to be put to work in order for your life to present a smooth and desirable finish to all who behold it. And believe me, in order to wear life well, your faith needs to be firmly rooted, tight, and secure.

What Does Faith Do?

Faith has several different functions.

Faith Compels Action

Although faith establishes and grounds you, it is also active. Faith compels the one who has it to do something. Without activity, faith is stagnant, and stagnation leads to death. Hence the quote from the Master Architect's Blueprint that "faith without works is dead" (James 2:26 NASB).

Faith Grows

It should be constantly increasing as we obey God. Working out is a good analogy for the process of growing faith. When you make your muscles experience resistance, those muscles begin to get bigger and stronger. The end result is something beautiful to behold, but it can be a painful process. It's true of building up bodies and building up one's faith: no pain, no gain.

Faith Beautifies

The trying of your faith, that resistance you feel when you embark on a new venture or determine to take life to the next level, will work to create perseverance or patience in you: "The testing of your faith produces endurance" (James 1:3 NASB). This patience becomes the voice of experience in your life. After a while you don't get as upset at seeming setbacks because you've experienced the pattern of progress. This experience fuels you with hope that you will overcome any hindrances, delays, or distresses and ultimately prevail.

You persist and never give up. Faith ultimately keeps you from being ashamed by failure and foolish, rash actions during times of crisis. In the end you have a beautiful work produced by faith! Paul referred to the Thessalonians' "work of faith and labor of love and steadfastness of hope in our Lord Jesus Christ" (1 Thess. 1:3 NASB)—could anything be more beautiful than that?

Faith Deflects Attacks

Faith also works as a shield, deflecting the things that attempt to assault your life and stop it from working: things such as fear, discouragement, doubt, ill health, financial setbacks, offense—you name it—anything that sets you off and keeps you from advancing in building a great life. These are the weapons the enemy of your soul uses to shut you down. The shield of faith (Eph. 6:16) repels his attempts and extinguishes the fiery darts he throws your way, taking the sting out of the things that could cause you to throw in the towel.

For example, after a friend or spouse offends you, only faith can restore your relationship. Your belief that things can be worked out and get better enables you to do the work required to restore your love for one another.

Faith Generates Strength

Faith can heal the sick when you get a gloom-and-doom report from the doctor. It is faith that makes you stay on a job you don't like—you believe you will get your check at the end of the week, no matter how mean your boss is. In the face of adversity and trial, faith makes you go against the grain of what you think, feel, and see. It does not allow you to listen to the negatives but helps you focus on the power of the original Architect of your life.

Perhaps this is why you have to "contend earnestly" for your faith at times (Jude 1:3 NASB). Fight for it! Without it, you wither and abdicate the life that works. Without this pillar, your ceiling and walls will crumble, and your house will fall in on itself.

Faith Helps Us Please God

In and of ourselves, in our finite humanity, we are just not wired to *do* right of our own volition. It is faith that empowers us to please God (Heb. 11:6). A friend of mine is quick to say, "If people knew better, they would do better." I'm not so sure about that. We all know better. Right and wrong are written onto our hearts from the beginning of time (Rom. 2:14–15). We instinctively know right from wrong because we were designed that way by the Master Creator and Architect.

Sometimes, though, we let our flesh drown out the voice of God's inner leading. If we do this long enough—if we opt to please ourselves rather than God—our consciences become "seared with a hot iron" (1 Tim. 4:2 NKJV). Such people "profess that they know God; but in works they deny him, being abominable, and disobedient, and unto every good work reprobate" (Titus 1:16 KJV). These faithless people no longer feel the prick of conviction the Holy Spirit uses to keep them in line with God's design. So many begin to rationalize, justify, and even deny that what they are doing is wrong.

Faith Works by Love

Paul wrote, "What is important is faith expressing itself through love" (Gal. 5:6). It is our love for God that makes us want to please Him. Our goal becomes more about pleasing Him than getting what we want. Still—when He is pleased, we usually do get what we want, because we want what He wants! This love makes us trust that if we do things according to the Master Blueprint, life will work as it should. We *will* triumph over the enemy. We *will* build lives that work and produce good fruit.

Love makes us trust our Beloved. We believe everything the One we love has to say. Because of this, we choose to obey His Word. When we obey His Word, we avoid the consequences of our disobedience and find that life is good. We begin to see the relevance and wisdom of His instructions and embrace them with joy—and love.

Your Role

With this in mind, know that you must add to faith in order for it to increase and grow stronger. The Blueprint gives us instruction for how to do this:

> Make every effort to supplement your faith with virtue, and virtue with knowledge, and knowledge with self-control, and self-control with steadfastness, and steadfastness with godliness, and godliness with brotherly affection, and brotherly affection with love. For if these qualities are yours and are increasing, they keep you from being ineffective or unfruitful in the knowledge of our Lord Jesus Christ. (2 Peter 1:5–8 ESV)

Now that is a mouthful! Peter, one of the Architect's highly skilled contractors, is saying that we boost our faith by adding these elements—virtue, knowledge, self-control, and so on—to the mix of our lives. These elements reinforce faith so you can withstand any pressure, assault, or wear and tear that you might face.

Let's look at these seven elements in a little more depth.

1. Virtue

Virtue, or moral excellence, sets you on the path of receiving good things because you've made a stand and determined to do things God's way: "For the LORD God is a sun and shield; the LORD bestows favor and honor. No good thing does he withhold from those who walk uprightly" (Ps. 84:11 ESV). Your decision to conduct your life a certain way bolsters and reaffirms your faith. Your determination to obey God actually fuels your faith—so choose to obey.

2. Knowledge
The more knowledge you have about God and about why you believe what you believe, the more you secure your faith and render it immovable.

3. Self-Control
Your knowledge can only strengthen your self-control because you refuse to be ruled by your emotions and lusts. If you believe the Word of God, you know the outcome of destructive and sinful actions and understand the motivation for God's instructions, so you avoid them.

4. Steadfastness
As you make a habit of regularly obeying God, your faith will be strengthened by steadfastness, or perseverance.

5. Godliness
After a while, going against what you know and believe will be going against the grain of who you are. Godliness should become a part of your DNA! You should find it harder to do bad things because doing good things has become so ingrained in you.

6. Brotherly Affection
Faith as a habit will give you a greater sense of self—more confidence in who and whose you are. Your confidence frees you to exercise brotherly (or sisterly) affection.

Godliness should become a part of your DNA!

7. Love

Brotherly affection matures into a deeper love. Love gives you the power to offer grace to all you encounter because you choose to believe the best of them.

When you look at all the qualities we use to supplement our faith, you can see why it is impossible to please God without faith. So many other qualities feed into faith, if one link suffers, the rest collapse with it. Then faith as a pillar becomes unstable and unsubstantial.

The seven supplements (some of which we will look at again on a deeper level in the Maintenance section) stabilize our faith and furnish us with the creative energy we need to be fruitful and productive in all we attempt.

In the Bible, seven is a significant number symbolic of perfection. Maturing and completing our faith with these seven supplements, simply put, makes us godly and gives us the power to build lives that work wonderfully. Our faith truly becomes a pillar on which the rest of the house can stand. If you have nothing to lean on, again, the structure of your life will collapse. And that, my friend, will just not work when it comes to life.

CONSTRUCTION TIP
Do not attempt to build your life without faith.
It will be shaky—at best—without it.

Health

Your health is essential to life's working for you. There are four aspects of health you need to consider: physical, mental, emotional, and spiritual. Let's look at these one at a time.

Physical Health

Many years ago I was hit by a car, injuring my leg very badly. After a year and a half in bed and a series of operations, let me tell you, life was difficult at best. The inability to walk put a serious kink in the simplest tasks and affected my ability to work, which in turn affected me financially and even relationally.

One event—one affected area of life—had a dramatic consequence on my overall existence. My social life shrank considerably. I couldn't go out, so I missed a lot of things.

I was happily surprised to find that all of my friends were committed to me; they all came alongside during my long climb back to health and mobility. They supported me with their care, their time, and even their resources. The guy I was seeing, however, was not able to deal with the situation at all. He was not interested in someone who was what he termed "sedentary."

So as you can see, one issue with my physical health affected the other pillars of my life: my profession, my ability to make money, and even my relationships, causing a domino effect that left me scrambling to recover my life and get back on track. At that point, because one part of me was not working, other things in my life had to be put on hold and my life overall stalled. There was a high level of discomfort—far beyond what I was used to and certainly above what I wished for myself. Thus, the point is your health affects more than you know.

The Master Architect has given us a detailed health regimen in the Blueprint. He outlines the best foods to eat—and those to avoid (Leviticus and Deuteronomy). Keep in mind that your diet can affect your health on all levels. Eating the wrong things can make you bloated, depressed, sick, and unproductive. Eating food that is good for you gives you energy and empowers you to complete your goals. Remember that the law of momentum is crucial to good health. The use of energy releases more energy and keeps you feeling fit. If you do nothing, you will always feel like doing nothing—so get moving! (Before developing a new diet or exercise regimen, always consult your physician.)

Though we have doctors and sophisticated methods of health care, let's face it, our bodies still rule. No amount of money on Earth can assure your good health. If good health could be bought, people the world over would sell all they had to acquire it. Many try anyway, to no avail.

> If good health could be bought, people the world over would sell all they had to acquire it.

The Master Architect and Creator, who also happens to be the Great Physician, understands that good health physical, mental, emotional, and spiritual—is of paramount importance in order for our lives to work. We've just looked at how physical health is important. Now let's look at the other areas of health we need to heed as we work to build successful lives.

Mental Health

Let's start with the mind—our mental health. As one famous institution is quick to remind us, a mind is a terrible thing to waste. When our minds are messed up, our lives are messed up. The ability to focus, follow through, and even believe is so wrapped up in the thoughts that the mind dwells upon.

Your mind can either energize you or paralyze you. There is no such thing as good luck; I believe that a sound mind has a lot to do with our perspective and the choices we make in light of those perceptions. This is why the Divine Architect's Blueprint lends clarity by saying we have not been given a "spirit of fear; but of power, and of love, and of a sound mind" (2 Tim. 1:7 KJV).

Another translation states that we have been given the spirit of power, love, and "self-discipline" (NIV). Fear hinders us from moving forward because it makes us believe the opposite of what is true or possible. It has been said that the acronym for *fear* is False Evidence Appearing Real. If we believe a lie, we will act on a lie and get a response that convinces us that the lie is true.

For example: Say someone tells you, "You can't do it." If you believe you can't, you won't try. You may have had the ability to do that thing. But because you didn't attempt it, you never discovered you could! Make sense? A sound mind affects whether we move forward or come to a standstill in life. The Blueprint says, "As he thinketh in his heart, so is he" (Prov. 23:7 KJV). Our thoughts drive our actions.

We must discipline our minds in order to function well. Power, love, and discipline work together to keep the mind in mint condition. Feelings of helplessness can debilitate the mind, and then our lives fail to work well.

An often-made excuse for people committing crimes is the insanity defense: unstable mental health. "This person is not responsible for his actions, Your Honor. He is not mentally sound." Many have avoided the consequences of their actions because this factor can be hard to prove one way or another. No one lives inside the mind of another, so how do you qualify the soundness of a person's mental capacity?

Yet there are instructions in the Blueprint that give us clear clues on how to secure our minds and maintain mental health.

Capture Those Thoughts!

First, the Bible tells us to bring "every thought into captivity to the obedience of Christ" (2 Cor. 10:5 NKJV). We have more control over our minds than we think!

As a child I was always reminded that I could not stop a bird from flying over my head, but I could stop it from building a nest in my hair! We are not supposed to allow our minds to run amuck. We must focus and master discipline. Bringing your thoughts and imaginations into subjection to God means you refuse to dwell on, accept, or consider any thoughts He does not agree with.

Make Them Good Thoughts

God does not want us to be mindless—thinking about nothing. He wants us to replace all negative thought with His positive thoughts. God sees the bigger picture—far beyond what we can see—and knows the final outcome, which always promises victory. This is why He tells us clearly what to think about so that our minds are strong and operate at their greatest capacity: "Whatever things are true...noble...just...pure...lovely...of good report, if there is any virtue and if there is anything praiseworthy—meditate on these things" (Phil. 4:8 NKJV).

Repeat these types of thoughts out loud in conversation and they begin to come to life, creating positive results in your life. This encourages you to think more good thoughts. These are the things that build up the mind and keep it sound. All of this is what makes the mind work.

Emotional Health

Depression can be damaging to a life or shut it down completely. The mind can play games with the emotions. If allowed to go unchecked, negative feelings can devastate a person's spirit. I've mentioned Proverbs 13:12, which says, "Hope deferred makes the heart sick, but when dreams come true, there is life and joy." There you have it: the lack of hope can slowly kill you but when hope is restored, you are brought back to life.

Elijah's Story: "Beam Me Up, Scotty"

The strongest person can be completely deflated by repeated experiences of disappointment, heartbreak, fear—whatever emotional expressions hardships cause. However, there is help for you. The Blueprint tells us that once upon a time there was a powerful prophet of God named Elijah. God gave him the ability to call down fire from heaven, hold up rain until he gave the word for it to fall, and outrun the king's chariot. In spite of all of this power, Elijah plummeted into the pit of depression after one woman threatened him.

Shortly thereafter we find Elijah laid out in the wilderness under a bush, asking God to take his life (or as I like to say, "Beam me up, Scotty"): "I have had enough, LORD," he said. "Take my life" (1 Kings 19:4).

Physical fatigue and emotional stress had shut down God's prophet. God sent an angel to feed him and allowed him to rest for a while. Then Elijah explained the despair he felt: "I have zealously served the LORD God Almighty. But the people of Israel have broken their covenant with you....I alone am left, and now they are trying to kill me, too" (1 Kings 19:10).

What interests me about this story is that God never chastised Elijah for feeling the way he did. God did not consider Elijah's feelings a breach or a failure of faith. He understood that Elijah was exhausted. He knew the prophet needed time away to rebuild his reserves before he was capable of doing any more work. This is the way the Master Architect has designed us. (The end of Elijah's story, by the way, is that he eventually triumphed over the woman—and everyone—who threatened him. He was restored to fulfill his purpose as God's prophet.)

Avoid Overload: Take Time to Recharge

Imagine a fuse box in the center of your being (every house has one, you know). It monitors how much you can bear. Once you've endured a great amount of stress, whether physical or emotional, the switch flips to slow you down before your overloaded circuits explode! The part you have to watch is that you don't stay down—you must reset the breaker switch (restore your tired body and soul) by feeding on God's Word and allowing His Spirit to refresh you. Then you can get back up and running.

When your mind and body are insisting you need to rest a while, heed them. Be honest with God about your exhaustion and the reasons for it. Let Him minister rest to you. Then you, like Elijah, can go back to fulfilling your God-given purpose.

Don't Let Feelings Lead

Another aspect of emotional health is deciding which is in charge: your mind or your emotions. Acting according to how you feel is not conducive to life working. Our actions should lead our emotions. Ever noticed that when you didn't feel like working out but did anyway, as soon as you got started you felt much better? As a matter of fact, you began to enjoy yourself! This is why choice is so powerful. Your choices should never be led by emotions alone. You must be mentally engaged in your decisions in order for life to work.

If left to run amuck, your emotions can even affect your physical health, causing lethargy, ulcers, headaches, all manner of ailments. The Blueprint says, "A relaxed attitude lengthens life; jealousy rots it away" (Prov. 14:30). On the flip side, a heart at peace gives life. Choosing joy over sadness empowers you to embrace good health.

Try this exercise. Put a big smile on your face and then say, "Oh, I am so depressed." Can't do it, can you? Because "a cheerful look brings joy to the heart" (Prov. 15:30). Your decision coupled with your physical stance cancels out the negative emotion and replaces it with the one of your choice.

The power to override what your emotions try to dictate is totally in your hands. The Master Architect is well aware of the importance of good emotional health in order for life to work and encourages healthy doses of joy and peace. He actually prescribes good cheer as medicine: "A merry heart does good, like medicine, but a broken spirit dries the bones" (Prov. 17:22 NKJV).

Note: If you find yourself continually stressed-out or depressed, seek professional help. It could be physiological. The Master Architect also uses physicians to help those He loves!

Spiritual Health

Spiritual health is also critical in the pursuit of a life that works well. This is why the Master Architects desires, as the apostle John put it, "that you may prosper in all things and be in health, *just as your soul prospers*" (2 John 1:3 NKJV, italics added). Our spiritual health has a lot to do with our overall health.

When we are in touch with our Divine Creator and Master Architect, we realize that our bodies are His temple. Therefore, we take better care of ourselves from the inside out. We have a healthy respect for our bodies. But we also nurture our spirits. Good spiritual health affects every choice we make: from the money we spend to the food we eat to the relationships we get involved in—literally everything. When we have grounded ourselves—established our foundations upon and submitted ourselves to the Master Architect of life—our knowledge of His Blueprint coupled with our personal love for Him helps us make the right choices, do the right things, and finally get the type of life we truly want: a life that works.

※

So you see, good health—physical, mental, emotional, and spiritual—has everything to do with how our lives work. Why is this important? Because in order for life to work for you at its best, everything about you must be working.

CONSTRUCTION TIP
Your health is something you should
guard with your life!

Profession

Your profession is an expression of your purpose, which we discussed earlier. This one area can create utter misery or genuine bliss. Many people hate to wake up in the morning because they hate going to work. I've been there, done that, and will never visit that country again. I have enough memories of bleak scenes of a job that I did not like, that I was not created to do, and that was finally my undoing. Remember, you will never be excellent at what you do not love. And you cannot love doing what you were not created to do.

This is why it is crucial to your existence to locate your gifts, then find your call and profession within the things that feed you and give you life and joy. There is nothing worse than doing a job that drains the life from you. Your work is supposed to feed you, not just financially but emotionally and spiritually, as well.

Jesus Knew His Profession

Jesus knew what His assignment was on Earth, what He was "built" to do: to spread the good news of reconciliation between God and man. He spent all of His time walking and talking with people about this one

You will never be excellent at what you do not love.

thing. Many thought He would make a great politician, but He stayed in His God-given role, doing what He loved, touching the needy and the broken.

Jesus was not interested in those who thought they had it all together, and He did not allow Himself to be distracted by them. He did not make Himself miserable arguing with them, thereby cutting down on His productivity. He focused on those who were hungry for truth and fed them life-giving secrets.

I am sure that when He laid His head down at night, He went to sleep with a sigh of not only contentment, but fulfillment. After all, He had spent the entire day doing the thing He loved most—reaching the lost, setting the captive free.

A perfect example of this is the story found in John 4. Jesus met a certain woman at a well in Samaria. The conversation they had that day revolutionized that woman's life and was the catalyst for her evangelizing an entire city. Many came to the saving knowledge of Christ because of her testimony of her encounter that day.

Meanwhile, Jesus' disciples had left him in search of food. Upon their return they urged Him to refresh Himself and eat something, but He told them, "I have food to eat of which you do not know" (John 4:32 NKJV). In other words, what had taken place that afternoon had been so nourishing to His soul, He was so full from the experience, He did not need natural food to satisfy him at that moment. The disciples didn't get it. He explained, "My food is to do the will of Him who sent Me, and to finish His work" (John 4:34 NKJV).

Whose work? The work of His Father. The One who created all of us. As sons and daughters of God, we are called to imitate Christ (that is what the word *Christian* means—"Christ-follower") and continue the work of God on Earth. We are to finish what He started, which is to be fruitful and productive in whatever field we find ourselves in.

Your Profession Should Bring
Revelation and Delight

As you strive to complete the work placed in your hands, you should find delight and fulfillment in it. If you are an administrator, you should be thriving on the details of your work, flourishing as you supervise others with grace and authority. If you are an artist, your creativity—the things God has placed within you to express—should surprise you!

No matter what your profession, it should reveal your strengths to you—as well as your weaknesses, the areas that could use improvement and refining. All of this is how we bless others and glorify God as we grow into a greater reflection of His creative power. Understanding that we are literally the extension of God's arms to the world is huge. Our inherent talents or gifts actually make up the expression of His care for those on Earth.

As I mentioned in the Purpose section, this is why we are called to exercise authority and maintain order within our sphere of influence and subdue the works of the evil one in the lives of others as well as ourselves (Gen. 1:28). God wants us to be standard-bearers.

Whether you are a receptionist, stay-at-home mom, doctor, lawyer, painter, janitor, singer, or fireman, how you live your life and express what God has placed in you will speak volumes about you and the God you serve. So make Him look good! Find the profession for which He created you, and thrive in it!

As Always, Consult the Master Architect

Many opt out of doing what God created them for because they can't figure out how to sustain themselves financially doing what they love.

Here is where you must confer with the Master Architect to get the full details of your personal design.

Some like to cook; perhaps they should consider becoming chefs, caterers, or food stylists for television commercials and shows. Some people like to shop. Do you know how much money personal shoppers make? There are lots of unique professions; don't be afraid to find out what really gives you and God pleasure. Where there is a will, there is a way to do what sets your heart on fire and make a living at the same time. This is what entrepreneurship is all about—creative ways to make a profession out of what you love doing.

If I've struck a chord with you, and you're wondering how to get from where you are to where you want to be, consider a realistic transition. Perhaps while you are on that practical job you must have in order to eat and pay the mortgage, you can begin your own business on the side. Then, when the demand for your talent rises to the point you can pay your bills by using your gift full-time, you can make the transition. (Note: this is a very *general* approach to being in business for yourself.)

When I wrote my first book, I was still working freelance as a writer of commercials. I did this for several years, until my book royalties and speaking engagements accrued to what was enough to sustain me financially. The turning point for me was when I asked the Lord if He truly wanted me to write and speak full-time—and if He did, to make a way for me to transition out of advertising.

Shortly after that, I landed a job doing a voice-over for an Extra gum television commercial. This commercial ran and ran, and the residuals made it possible for me to phase out of my advertising work and concentrate fully on doing what I truly loved: empowering men and women to live, love, and overcome in their everyday lives.

I've never looked back. Every day I'm elated and a bit in awe of the fact that someone has been helped by what I have to offer. I have to say, at the end of the day, what I do feels like a big box of goodies that

God gave me to enjoy! Yes, your profession should be a pillar that supports you financially—but also emotionally and spiritually.

If you don't feel great about the work you do, it is time to find something new, something more in keeping with what God made you for. If you're not enjoying yourself, the quality of your work is slipping. I can tell you this from experience!

And you may not be the only one who is miserable. Your employer is probably just as, if not more, miserable than you! End the torture for both of you: if you long in your heart of hearts to be elsewhere doing something else, own that fact. Consult the Master Architect for building instructions. And find a profession that fits your gift and go for it.

What *Are* My Gifts?

By now you may be saying, "That is just the problem, Michelle—I don't know what my gifts are!" Let me help you with that. I've said it in practically every book I've written: your gift is the thing that everyone around you celebrates but you take for granted because it comes so easily to you. That's why it's called a *gift*. Everyone can't do it the way you do. It's something you love doing. It's how you express yourself. This is the thing that you will be excellent at and it will be your entree into where you really want to go. Proverbs 18:16 says, "A man's gift makes room for him, and brings him before great men" (NKJV). Another translation puts it this way: "A gift opens the way for the giver and ushers him into the presence of the great" (NIV). Great men are always willing to applaud and pay for excellence.

A hint to your profession is what gets a rise out of you. What makes you excited, or even angry? What makes you put your hand on your hip and say, "Somebody ought to do something about that"? That somebody is probably you! If you have the burden, God will give you the solution, and your passion for the matter will fuel your drive to address that specific need.

This is the secret to your purpose and your success. Success will give you joy. Nothing is more delightful than being able to make a living doing what you love. It almost feels criminal, as if it shouldn't be possible to have such a great time in life!

Now take that gift and use it. Channel what it has to offer to bless others and prosper yourself. When a gift is used to benefit more than the recipient in the form of your profession, life works for everyone. That is called living a life worthy of your calling (Eph. 4:1)!

Consider Mother Teresa, Martin Luther King Jr., those called to practice law, medicine, or even to write a book. Their passions became their profession. Passion must be honed, harnessed, and refined with knowledge, understanding, and compassion to work as it should (Prov. 19:2). When this occurs, you build a beautiful house/life that works to better the lives of countless others.

CONSTRUCTION TIP
In order to bolster your profession pillar, utilize your gifts and passions. Place them appropriately and they will work for you.

Finances

When it comes to building and sustaining the life you want, money is one of the most powerful parts of the equation. When writing his ecclesiastical dissertation, King Solomon said that "money is a shelter" (Eccl. 7:12 NIV). On another occasion, he commented wryly that "money is the answer for everything" (Eccl. 10:19 NIV).

Of course we know that is not true. Just take a look at all the problems money can cause and the lives it has ruined. You've seen them on television—the wealthy people who are still miserable because their money only bought them more problems or they became obsessed with obtaining more. The Master's Blueprint speaks about that: "Whoever loves money never has money enough; whoever loves wealth is never satisfied with his income" (Eccl. 5:10 NIV).

How do we find the balance so we have money, but money doesn't have us? How do we keep money from putting our lives in precarious positions? How do we make it work for us in life instead of against us? How do we get and keep the right perspective so that our finances become a pillar in our lives—something that stabilizes us and frees us to be the blessing that we should be to others?

A Guide to Money

Here are a few steps to making money a tool rather than a taskmaster.

Know That It Is Not Your Money!

Everything, including your money, belongs to God. He's just nice enough to let you use some of it. Favor and "promotion" come from Him; so does "the power to get wealth" (Ps. 75:6–7 KJV; Deut. 8:18 NKJV). As a matter of fact, we should be aware that when God gives anyone "wealth and possessions, and enables him to enjoy them, to accept his lot and be happy in his work—this is a gift from God" (Eccl. 5:19 NIV).

Know the Difference between Riches and Wealth

Many overlook the far more desirable gift of wealth and get caught up in the race to attain riches, thinking cash will solve all their problems. Riches are one thing—the actual dollars. But being able to enjoy riches in your right mind, with your health intact, surrounded by love and flourishing relationships, thriving in your purpose, living at peace with your God, and above all things, being so free from what you possess that if you lost it all tomorrow nothing would change at the center of your core—now that is wealth!

Knowing that there is something more important than temporal acquisitions and living with the mind-set that the eternal holds far greater joy and fulfillment keeps you from the bondage in which greed can entrap you. For the love of money, the O'Jays sang, people would do just about anything in order to gain that "mean green."

Know How to Have It but Not Love It

The basic guideline is to keep yourself "free from the love of money and be content with what you have"—to have it but not love it (Heb.

13:5 NIV). "The love of money is a root of all kinds of evil" (1 Tim. 6:10 NIV). Even in ministry, people often sacrifice their integrity when they build ministries far beyond their capacity to sustain them. The apostle Paul wrote, "People who want to get rich fall into temptation and a trap and into many foolish and harmful desires that plunge men into ruin and destruction" (1 Tim. 6:9 NIV).

The monster named *More* grows larger, its appetite consuming everything in sight. This is when the trouble begins and God's reputation gets smeared: men and women act from fear to maintain what they created. Remember that not every good idea is a God idea. With the vision He gives, He also gives provision to finish the work He has asked you to begin.

Know the Dangers of Too Much *or* Too Little

One of the top reasons for crime as well as marital failure has to do with finances—either the lack of or too much of them. On the one hand, the lack of money can wear on partners who find themselves struggling with debt. Whether the debt rose out of what the couple viewed as necessity or simply from trying to keep up with the Joneses, it can really stymie a life or a love life.

On the other hand, having too much causes many to avoid the rigors and exercises of life that create sound character. For example, perhaps the marriages in Hollywood (and elsewhere) don't last because both parties can afford to leave. Back when only one member of the union was working, a spouse thought long and hard before bailing out because there were great financial ramifications. Today the attitude is, "I don't need you and I can afford to leave!" This is the age of "no-fault divorce," a truly ironic statement.

> You can be monetarily wealthy yet spiritually and emotionally bankrupt.

Know What God Wants

I've mentioned that the Master Architect wants you to "prosper and be in good health, *just as your soul prospers*" (3 John 1:2 NASB, italics added). Financial wealth must be balanced with spiritual prosperity in order for life to work as it should. You can be monetarily wealthy yet spiritually and emotionally bankrupt.

The Blueprint on Finances

Prosperity comes in many forms and manifests itself in every other pillar in the frame of your life. Only you can be honest about the richness of your intimate relationships. Only you know if your spiritual journey and relationship with God are growing and life-giving, whether you abound physically with good health, whether you are fruitful and productive in your work, whether you handle your money in such a way that it is growing for you and freeing you to be generous with God and others in need.

Wealth, my friend, begins within. It begins in your being at peace with yourself and God, in having all of your relationships reconciled, in having your health and your strength. No amount of money can buy you these things.

On the other hand, you need to know how to use the riches (cash) that God allows you to enjoy. It is amazing that everyone in the world needs and uses money but few have a healthy respect for it or know how to use it properly. Many books can guide you in how to build and manage your finances, so I will give you just the basics from the Blueprint—then you can pick and choose wisely from the instructions the plethora of financial advisors will give you.

The Secret of the Tithe

The secret to having all your needs met—the operative word being *needs*—is very simple. It is the secret of the tithe. We are to give our firstfruits or the first tenth of our increase of earnings back to the One who originates and graciously provides—that would be God. Talk about an insurance plan! This is one of the guarantees straight out of the Blueprint:

> "Bring the whole tithe into the storehouse, that there may be food in my house. Test me now in this," says the LORD Almighty, "and see if I will not throw open the floodgates of heaven and pour out so much blessing that you will not have room enough for it. I will prevent pests from devouring your crops, and the vines in your fields will not cast their fruit," says the LORD Almighty. "Then all the nations will call you blessed." (Malachi 3:10–12 NIV)

Broken down into everyday language, this passage says: take care of the things God is concerned about—having a storehouse (a church or place available to those who are hungering and thirsting for righteousness) where people can go for sustenance. Such people can find help whenever they need it because those who have brought their tithes and offerings facilitate feeding the broken, needy, and hungry.

God's Provision for You

If you do this, God will guard your money for you! What you don't receive in the form of money you will receive in the form of provision—don't get confused on this. Sometimes we think God should do things one way and He, another. He might not give you the money to buy something that you want, but He might just touch someone to buy it for you.

The bottom line is that God will provide for you in very creative ways. Just don't get confused about the true source. The moment you think you are creating and increasing wealth, you are in trouble. You are heading toward an enlightening moment. One king, who got a big head, lost his compassion for the poor, and thought he had accomplished everything by his own strength and genius, found himself humbled and eating grass (Dan. 4:33, 5:21)!

God Will Sustain You

When God said in Malachi, "I will prevent pests from devouring your crops," He meant you won't be wiped out again and again by unexpected emergencies (v. 11 NIV). Those are the kind of "pests" I'm talking about: the robbers that keep you perpetually in financial recovery mode. The Master Architect has designed your financial pillar to be strengthened every time you choose to give, understanding that it is more blessed to give than to receive.

When you value spiritual things first—heeding what God says about widows, orphans, the disenfranchised, and those who take care of the house of God—He will return the favor by supplying all of your needs out of His own personal storehouse of riches in glory by Christ Jesus (Phil. 4:19).

Deal with the Spiritual First

If we can just fulfill our internal need or hunger, we won't have so many external needs or hungers. God encourages us to "seek first his kingdom and his righteousness"—satisfying our internal or spiritual need for right standing with the Master Architect of our lives—and He will supply all of the external or material things we need (Matt. 6:33 NIV). He can trust us with all of the add-ons *after* we have dealt with our spiritual need. We will own our possessions, but our possessions will not own us. We will see the value and beauty of giving it all away for a cause greater than ourselves.

The saying goes, "The rich get richer while the poor get poorer." Perhaps this is true because the rich give away a lot of their money.

It doesn't matter what the motivation is: the more you give, the more you get. It is the law of the universe whether you choose to embrace God or not.

It is on this premise alone that your financial pillar will be immovable and unaffected by any external elements—the stock market, the price of real estate, even unemployment and recession. The law of reaping and sowing will continue to make life work for you.

CONSTRUCTION TIP
Finances, like life, don't really get good
until you are able to give them away.

Tools

- ❋ Wisdom
- ❋ Attitude
- ❋ Habits
- ❋ Character

The Rules for Tools

When building a life that works, you have to plan your work. After you've got your plan in place, complete with a picture of what you want your life to look like, it's time to get down to the real work. For this you need tools—serious tools that won't break or malfunction, that are available and effective no matter what you face in life. They should be weathered and strong; you will never be able to build a lasting structure with weak tools or material.

Tools are necessary to put anything together and keep it together. Some tools should be staples in your life; other specialized tools will be used only in cases of emergency situations such as broken relationships, financial struggles, health issues, and so on.

The four tools you must have at all times, no matter what you are going through, are wisdom, a right attitude, godly habits, and sound character. These will serve to realign, straighten, strengthen and keep the right things in place in your life and propel you toward your destiny—which will affect more lives than you can ever imagine. Keep these tools within easy grasp, use them well, and they will make life work for you.

Wisdom

Of course, you have to love the idea that wisdom is referred to as feminine in the Master Architect's Blueprint. But then again, perhaps I shouldn't get happy too quickly, since folly is also referred to as a woman. Interestingly, wisdom and folly are very similar, issuing the same invitation to the same group of people.

Wisdom...calls from the highest point of the city.
"Let all who are simple come in here!"
she says to those who lack judgment.
"Come, eat my food
and drink the wine I have mixed.
Leave your simple ways and you will live;
walk in the way of understanding." (Proverbs 9:1, 3–5 NIV)

The woman Folly is loud;
she is undisciplined and without knowledge.
She sits at the door of her house,
on a seat at the highest point of the city,
calling out to those who pass by,
who go straight on their way.
"Let all who are simple come in here!"
she says to those who lack judgment.

"Stolen water is sweet;

    food eaten in secret is delicious!" (Proverbs 9:13–17 NIV)

Both invitations sound good until you realize where each visit will end. One leads to (a well-built) life and the other leads to death and brokeness. Guess which is which. Wisdom declares, "Whoever finds me finds life and receives favor from the LORD. But whoever fails to find me harms himself; all who hate me love death" (Prov. 8:35–36 NIV). Wisdom not only promises and delivers the good life, she adds some pretty wonderful extras to the package: riches and honor, enduring wealth, and prosperity (Prov. 1:18).

Let's not skip over the extras too quickly. Notice that wisdom understands the difference between riches and wealth—which we covered in the last chapter. Riches refer to the material part of your life and can fluctuate or dissipate altogether, but wealth has to do with the quality of your life. Wealth includes the things that money cannot buy. These are the things the Master Designer wants to build into your life with unrivaled quality so the things that nurture your well-being are sustainable.

Spiritual prosperity helps you to see things from the Master Architect's point of view and design. This leads to a life of balance and order so that all you accumulate remains a blessing and does not turn into a curse for yourself or others. Wisdom is the catalyst for this because wisdom protects the lives of those who possess it (Eccl. 7:12).

Use Wisdom to Build and Sustain a Quality Life

In order for life to work with sustained quality, wisdom has to be at work in your life. What exactly is wisdom? It is knowledge with understanding. Zeal without knowledge is bad, but knowledge without understanding can also be crippling. If you have a lot of data but

> **S**ense is *not* common—it must be pursued and mastered.

no understanding, you are simply harboring information without knowing how, when, or why to apply it to your circumstances. This is why the Master Architect's Blueprint recommends, "Though it cost you all you have, get understanding" (Prov. 4:7 NIV).

Sense is *not* common—it must be pursued and mastered. Many who have not attained high levels of education have still made major strides in life because they had understanding. Some would call it *street smarts*, but I would call it *wisdom* one has attained from a healthy combination of observation and practical life lessons. When people couple what they've learned with a creative use of their innate gifts, they rise to the top in their fields of enterprise. Without wisdom built into the very fiber of your life, every area will be affected and need serious repair in no time flat!

Godly Wisdom and Worldly Wisdom

Let's differentiate between worldly and godly wisdom. People using the tool of godly wisdom have a pure motive. They don't operate from "bitter envy," "selfish ambition," or arrogance. These terms actually describe worldly wisdom (James 3:14 NIV). People who use the tool of worldly wisdom will always create disorder and chaos. Look at the motive behind the decision, no matter how brilliant the idea may seem. Selfishness rules out people's needs and hurts others.

But godly wisdom is gentle, reasonable, "full of mercy and good fruit," consistent, and without hypocrisy; therefore, it creates peace and peaceful outcomes in every situation (James 3:17 NIV). People with godly wisdom are always on their best behavior. They don't take advantage of another person's ignorance but always pursue what is good for everyone.

As I've said before, every idea is not necessarily a God idea. In other words, "There is a way that seems right to a man, but its end is the way of death" (Prov. 16:25 NKJV). This could be the death of the deal, of the relationship, of your joy—you name it.

Following our own inclinations is not always the wisest thing to do. This is why we must trust in the Lord and not depend on our own understanding—which is earthly and natural at best, far beneath godly wisdom. In all our ways we are to check in with Him, acknowledge Him, and allow Him to give us the Blueprint for life (Prov. 3:5–6). This is the foundation for making wise choices that bolster our spirits and give us the impetus to keep moving forward in life victoriously.

Sometimes there seems to be no road map or clear-cut path to where we want to go. This is why knowledge of the Holy One is so important. When we trust His leading, even when we can't see where He is taking us, we find that the plans He has for us are always for good.

Consider Abraham, who struck out for a land that he did not know. He simply moved out based solely on the instruction of God. Can you imagine him going to his wife and saying, "Baby, pack up the china. We're moving"? And when questioned on where, Abraham answered, "I don't know! God said go, so we're going!" (Gen. 12). Knowledge of the Holy told him the move was for his good, even though he didn't have the specifics. Wisdom directed him to follow the voice of God, and he became a wealthy man, as well as the father of many nations, for doing so without question or hesitance.

Again, Abraham didn't know everything when he left—in fact, he knew almost nothing about where he was going or what the plan was. But he left himself open to discover the rest, which God revealed along the way. This one factor probably garnered him more favor than he knew because he had nothing to flaunt but his awe of a God who blessed his life beyond his imagination.

Look at what the Blueprint says: "By faith Abraham, when he

was called, obeyed.... He was looking for the city *which has foundations, whose architect and builder are God*" (Heb. 11:8, 10 NASB, italics added). Here we're reminded of the importance of faith as a pillar, the foundation of our lives, and who is our Master Architect: the Lord God Himself.

Godly Wisdom Doesn't Hurt Anyone

We feel the pressure to accumulate data and facts, but sometimes knowing "everything" is not enough. Wisdom shows you how to apply your knowledge without offending or hurting others. Sometimes standing on principle, even though you are right, leaves you standing alone—because you were obnoxious in proving your point. This isn't wise at all. There is a difference between being a wise guy (girl) and walking in wisdom.

Wisdom promotes understanding between all involved in a situation because a wise person knows when to hold his or her peace. You cannot have understanding if you insist on standing over (dominating) someone. You must be willing to stand under him or her (take his or her interests into account) so that both of you are lifted to common ground. Then both parties are nurtured and satisfied by the outcome of the decision.

The writer of Proverbs said it best: "By wisdom a house is built, and by understanding it is established; and by knowledge the rooms are filled with all precious and pleasant riches" (24:3 NASB). By wisdom and understanding, a house (life) is built and established. By knowledge, "all precious and pleasant riches" accumulate in this house (life). These include rich relationships and fulfilling exchanges in the workplace, your community, and your personal realm. Everything you want to build in a life that works will depend on wisdom.

Pursuing peace through understanding will stabilize and secure your life. Wisdom will help you to walk straight. Based on what you know, you will acquire all your heart's desires as you make educated choices in the way you pursue love, success, financial gain, good health, and anything else on your list.

I sometimes wonder why it took me so long to accomplish some of the things on my wish list of many years ago. When I questioned God on this, He made it clear to me that He waited until I was equipped with enough knowledge, wisdom, and understanding to handle all I wanted. Wisdom comes with time and experience, through our trials, failures, triumphs, and even our mistakes.

Every single experience is part of the process the Master Architect uses to build wisdom into your internal system. You are not a fool for making a mistake—only for despising correction and refusing to learn from it. Foolishness can be the greatest robber of power in your life, while wisdom, when used as a tool, can be one of your greatest sources of empowerment.

This is a foundational truth when attempting to make life work: "A wise man is strong, and a man of knowledge increases power" (Prov. 24:5 NASB). Make sure you get a good grip on this most essential power tool.

CONSTRUCTION TIP
Do not attempt to make life work without wisdom.
Without this tool, nothing in your life
will come together.

Attitude

I t doesn't matter what you say—your actions reveal your true attitude toward life, yourself, and others. It has been said that attitude is everything, and it is...well, almost. It is another power tool that can make or break a life—that's for sure.

Your attitude determines your thoughts, words, and actions. Your actions invite specific responses that further solidify your attitude, which propels your next action, which invites the next response...whew! This can become a vicious cycle of defeat or lead to a systematic progression of success in every area of your life. As people think in their hearts, so are they—it's just that simple. Your attitude is the outward manifestation or reflection of who you are.

When making clearly destructive choices, people often say, "Well, God knows my heart." People say this to excuse their actions, yet the very things they do reveal exactly what thoughts, desires, and attitudes they really harbor in their hearts. There is no separation between your attitude and your actions. One compels the other.

Your Attitude Can Rob or Bless You

So how does your attitude work for you in life? Your attitude can generate actions that bear abundant fruit or render you completely ineffective and unfruitful.

Consider the story of the master who gave talents to three of his servants in Matthew 24. He considered the ability of each of his servants before he distributed five to one, two to another, and one to a third servant before he left on a lengthy journey.

Two of the servants believed the master was good and would reward them if they increased his investment. When the master returned, they were excited to share that they had doubled what he'd given them. The master, of course, celebrated their achievement.

But the third servant had a completely different attitude. He harbored animosity toward and fear of the master. Instead of pursuing anything that could have increased what he had, he chose to bury his talent for safekeeping. In the end he returned only what his initial portion had been.

This servant didn't trust his master to reward him. He abdicated responsibility for the talent left in his care. This displeased the master greatly. He called the servant wicked and lazy and took the one talent back and gave it to one of the other servants.

The moral of the story? Your attitude can rob you of tremendous blessings and set you up for unnecessary failure.

What This Means in the Twenty-First Century

This is why it is important to have faith as well as knowledge of God. If we truly know His heart, we should also know that He has distributed gifts to us according to His knowledge of our potential. We should never envy others but simply focus on what we have to share and strive to increase what we have. When we prove ourselves faithful with a little, we will be made rulers over much.

Don't miss this: doubting *our* ability is really doubting *God's* ability. We can do anything with God's help; the psalmist wrote, "In your strength I can crush an army; with my God I can scale any

Doubting *our* ability is really doubting *God's* ability.

wall" (18:29). If that is true, self-doubt has no place in our minds. Our faith should never be in ourselves anyway. The Blueprint tells us, "It is not by force nor by strength"—natural power or might—that anything is accomplished, "but by my Spirit" as we follow His instructions (Zech 4:6).

All thinking not conducive to victorious living must be trashed. Now you cannot get rid of something without replacing it with something else. As I mentioned earlier, this is why the Master Architect instructs us on what we *should* think about (see Phil. 4:8). Let these good thoughts reshape your attitude.

What Makes Up Your Attitude— and Your Destination

You will attract what you are as well as what you believe you deserve. (This, by the way, is simply the law of God, firmly established in the universe.) Your beliefs can be determined by what your parents or others taught you. You may also solidify an attitude based on a series of positive or negative experiences. This is why it is important to examine whether the attitude you hold—or what you believe you deserve—is objectively true or based on an emotional experience. Remember that emotions are responses, not a reliable analysis of the issue you are dealing with.

Attitude can also be colored by motive, so purity of your agenda is essential when it comes to separating fact from fiction. If you focus on the positive instead of the negative, that is what you will not only attract but pursue. Your body will follow what you believe and lead you into places that will assist you in getting what you want out of life.

If, however, you focus on the negative and believe only the worst about yourself, you will get only what you *do not* want and weave a tale of woe that includes blaming others, not taking ownership of your life, and wallowing in a pool of regret. Doing away with fear, anger, doubt, and unbelief is essential for the right attitudes to take root and bear fruit in your life.

You see, you have to make room for right thoughts, embrace what is really true. You are loved. You are valuable. You do have something to contribute to your community—to the world! Yes, this is what is true, so conduct yourself that way. Your mind determines your attitude, and your attitude determines your destination.

Two Attitudes That Can Ruin Your Life

What is honorable, what is praiseworthy, what nurtures a grateful heart—these will create a great attitude and a great outcome in this life you are building. Even the world gets this—it's no secret. But either of two major attitudes can, if you make them part of every day and every thought, demolish your hopes for a life that works. Let's look at these.

1. The Attitude of Entitlement

If you are stuck in bad-attitude mode, a deep truth must be acknowledged: an idol is taking up residence in your heart. "What idol?" you ask. The idol of how you think your life should be and isn't, what you should have acquired by now but haven't, what God should have done for you but didn't—or worse yet, what He should not have allowed but did. It's all about *you* and your desires rather than yielding to the Master Architect's Blueprint for your life whether you understand it all or not.

When we begin to idolize the life we want and remain bitter because it has not appeared, we cling to wrong thoughts and ungrateful murmurings and miss what is present to celebrate right here, right now. This type of self-indulgence sends our lives further on the downward spiral. An attitude of entitlement declares we are due so much more than we have.

It is impossible to stop that spiral *unless* you are committed to making a drastic inward change. As Jonah said in the belly of the fish, after having three days to think about it, "Those who cling to worthless idols forfeit the grace that could be theirs" (Jon. 2:8 NIV). Put another way: "Those who worship false Gods turn their backs on all God's mercies." If you are so distracted by what is not presently in place in your life, you cannot see and celebrate the blessings, the "mercies," you *do* have. Attitude is the tool you can use to escape the destruction negativity can bring. A grateful heart sets the stage for greater blessings.

2. The Attitude of Victimization

Many years ago, I took a trip to Florida. Once in my room, I heard a disturbing, continuous noise. I knew I wouldn't get any sleep if I stayed there, so I dragged my bags back down to the front desk and switched rooms. Once I was safely ensconced in my second room, I noticed the same irritating noise. This time I was tired and annoyed, so I called the front desk to complain. They were most apologetic, this time sending a bellman to help me move to yet another room. As a matter of fact, this time they put me in a suite to make up for my trouble. After I settled in once again, the noise returned. I couldn't believe it!

I began walking around the room, trying to find the source of the noise. The closer I got to my toiletry suitcase, the louder it became. I was mortified to learn it was my electric toothbrush happily churning away in the bottom of my bag. The frustration had been no one's fault but my own.

Are you getting this? Sometimes it's not everybody else. Sometimes your problem developed only because of you. You are the source of your own pain, shame, or undesirable situation. Claiming the attitude that you are always the victim, never the victor, creates a dysfunctional life. A person who believes she is always a victim of other people's malicious intent or bullying will never have a life that works. In every repeated cycle you must be aware that the common denominator is you. So check yourself. Check your attitude.

An Attitude with Which to Build Life

It's time to flip the script. What should the right attitude be? "I can do all things through Christ who strengthens me" (Phil. 4:13 NKJV). You can be loved. Productive. An overcomer! "All" means *all*.

Say these words out loud:

> In the meantime I will be grateful for where I am, who I am, and whose I am. I will develop an attitude of gratitude. I will focus on the positive, accept the negative, and put it in the right perspective. I will rejoice in all things, counting them as one more step closer to getting the life I want. And if I don't feel it the first time I try to rejoice, I will rejoice again until I can get to a place of authentic praise in order to release new strength in my being. I will see even my setbacks as opportunities to learn yet one more priceless lesson that will assist me in moving forward and building a life that works.

When you can say this in genuine earnestness, you will see the salvation of the Lord at work in your life in every area. And that, my friend, will make life work for you as it should.

CONSTRUCTION TIP
If you find yourself stuck or failing to function in life as you should, check your attitude—if you need a new tool, by all means, get it!

Habits

Some tools will make or break your life. The habits you cultivate are one of them. Like power screws that can either secure a mechanism or break it if adjusted too tightly, habits can either set you on your course for success or send you spiraling into the abyss of failure.

Habits are the disciplines in your life that dictate your final outcome. Athletes, for example, are in the habit of working out, of eating a certain way, of avoiding specific actions or even people and places that do not help them build the stamina and strength needed for their sports. They develop regimens that keep them focused for the final test or game. Athletes prepare themselves for going the distance.

In life, it is the same: your habits will help you go the distance or fall short of your goals. Habits lock you into a direction and keep you on course. Without them, life becomes a loosey-goosey affair that never quite comes together or holds any degree of lasting substance. When you live without discipline, you are going with the flow—and going absolutely nowhere. Remember, in every success story you will ever read or witness, someone's consistent habits were the anchor of his or her success.

Four Kinds of Habits That Keep Life Working

There are several brands of the habit tool—spiritual, mental, verbal, and physical—and each one is equally important. Each plays an important role in how your life will operate. Let's examine these one at a time.

Spiritual Habits

Spiritually speaking, you must have a routine—even Jesus had one. He sought the Father in intimate prayer (Luke 5:16, 6:12; Mark 1:35). In the world, some refer to this as "centering" themselves. Others insist they need to hear from on high before they begin their day. I second the motion.

Every job in life has systems, set routines that enable the workers to complete their tasks. Before people begin a project, for example, they receive their assignments. Life can be like a job. Getting direction and clear-cut steps to help you navigate is essential to your success. You've got to get your orders and know the parameters of your project before you can set the wheels in motion for anything you want to accomplish in life. Who better to consult than the One who made you and knows how you work—as well as how everything else works?

You need input from the One who has a bird's-eye view of your situation; the One who can see all the ins and outs, the possible hazards as well as the easiest routes to take. With God's clear direction, you are destined for success in every area of your life, but you must take the time to seek His wisdom. Creating the habit of being still, seeking His face, listening to His voice, and searching His Word is one of the greatest power tools you will ever use.

Not only is seeking God consistently a power tool, it is a restorative tool. The wear and tear of life makes regular restoration necessary. Movers and shakers know the importance of gaining direction, insight, and restoration from those more powerful than themselves. If you want to know how to run a country, why not consult the One who rules the world?

The king of Israel, David, said,

> God, you are my God,
> earnestly I seek you.
> ...My soul will be satisfied as with the richest of foods.
> ...I think of you through the watches of the night.
> ...You are my help. (Psalm 63:1, 5–7 NIV)

David saw God not only as his help but as the One who nurtured, fulfilled, and restored him. It's one thing to be full, but it is another to be satisfied. A consistent spiritual routine keeps every other area of your life on track. It becomes the axis from which everything else spins. Do not equate having good spiritual habits with being religious. Religion is deadly. We are not talking about going through the motions so you appear "spiritual." We are talking about cultivating a healthy relationship with the Master Architect of life. Regular consultation with Him is the key to gaining wisdom and revelation concerning the intricacies of your life.

> A consistent spiritual routine keeps every other area of your life on track.

There are some things only He knows. Friends and family can take you only so far with their suggestions, so make it your business to check in with the One who is able to give effective help in all matters. The more regular your time spent with Him, the less drama you will have in your life. Note: you will not be exempt from trouble, but you will be equipped to handle it.

Once you've established this important discipline of having a spiritual routine, five steps will make that habit a tool that gives you strength and power in your daily life.

Step 1: Die daily. You will have to sacrifice daily in order to get anywhere in life. Just to get across the road sometimes requires a sacrifice; for example, you have to patiently wait for the light to change before you can turn onto another street.

In short, get over yourself. Life is not all about you. It's about God first and everybody and everything second. Removing yourself and your perceived rights from the equation leaves room for much more happiness and fulfillment. Personal insistence will always kill your joy.

Dying daily—exchanging your wants and plans for God's—keeps you flexible and open to new directions that can lead to paths of pleasant surprises. C. S. Lewis entitled his autobiography *Surprised by Joy*. That says it all! But I think most people are not open enough to be surprised by joy. They are far too insistent on how their lives should go. This cuts off their options and hinders God from being able to do new and surprising things in their lives. Dying daily is an important part of your spiritual habit.

Step 2: Take up your cross. Shoulder your responsibilities with conviction and a sense of purpose. Some issues and events in life are painful but necessary. Handle them with dignity. All of us have crosses to bear. God has crafted your particular "cross" with precision to fit your shoulder, your strength. God will send help in those times when you stumble beneath the weight of it. Persevere, knowing a reward awaits you.

Part of the dying is acknowledging and submitting to the things that are necessary for true (abundant) life to blossom, not only for ourselves but for all who inhabit our world. Be willing to bear the weight and gravity of the issues of your life. This means making responsible choices that aren't necessarily fun but are worth their weight in gold later, or staying focused and disciplined when you would rather throw caution to the wind. These choices will work for you in the long run.

Step 3: Get dressed. Put on the armor God supplies so that when trouble comes, you will be able to stand your ground. Paul put it this way:

> God is strong, and he wants you strong. So take everything the Master has set out for you, well-made weapons of the best materials. And put them to use so you will be able to stand up to everything the Devil throws your way. This is no afternoon athletic contest that we'll walk away from and forget about in a couple of hours. This is for keeps, a life-or-death fight to the finish against the Devil and his angels.
>
> Be prepared. You're up against far more than you can handle on your own. Take all the help you can get, every weapon God has issued, so that when it's all over but the shouting you'll still be on your feet. Truth, righteousness, peace, faith, and salvation are more than words. Learn how to apply them. You'll need them throughout your life. (Ephesians 6:11–17 *The Message*)

Put on your helmet of salvation, your guarantee of life wearing well throughout eternity; the belt of truth, which will keep you on point and out of trouble, no ifs, ands, or buts about it; and the breastplate of righteousness, your defense against self-doubt as well as your entrée into the good graces of God. Be filled with the readiness that comes from being equipped with the gospel of peace. Know why you stand for what you stand for. Then grab the shield of faith and the sword of the Spirit so that you will be equipped to effectively battle the spiritual forces that consistently assault your mind, your body, and your spirit.

Step 4: Eat. You need to nourish your spirit as well as your body daily. Take just enough of a portion for this day—there is plenty more where that came from. No need to overstuff yourself and get constipated or stuck on one thing. There was a reason God instructed the children of Israel this way: "Then the LORD said to Moses, 'I will rain down bread from heaven for you. The people are to go out each day and gather enough for that day'" (Exod. 16:4 NIV). In other words, bite off only what you can chew and trust God for tomorrow's provision. This develops your dependence on Him and not yourself for sustenance and results in consistent peace in an ever-changing world. Thus the phrase, "Give us this day our daily bread."

Step 5: Grow daily. If you are not growing you are stagnating, which leads to death as sure as you're born. As you yield more and more of yourself to the One who made you, you will find yourself growing by leaps and bounds with so much more to contribute to others. Growth leads to greater productivity. Growing is good for you and for everyone around you!

Mental Habits

Remember that your thought life is the driver for all of your actions. You have to be able to shift into the right gear to move in the right direction. Dwelling on issues that prove only to be unworthy distractions or power robbers is not conducive to your gaining a momentum that can lead to a life that works.

We covered thoughts earlier, but I have to reiterate that you are in the position of power when it comes to your mind. It should not run you. You should run it. Do not allow the mind to run rampant—the end of the matter will be disaster. Stand at the helm of your mind and command it. Focus on life-giving thoughts—things that will be a blessing to yourself and others.

When something makes you angry, the more you think about it, the angrier you get, right? It is up to you in that moment to redirect your thought life. As you decisively take dominion of your thought life on a daily basis, you will find it becoming easier to stay in the right frame of mind.

Verbal Habits

Your mind-set will spill out into words. You can speak only what you are thinking. Yes, it's true that even in jest, a man or woman speaks "out of the abundance of the heart" (Luke 6:45 NKJV). The heart is the place that harbors our thoughts and attitudes. Umm-hmm, we literally speak our minds! Here is the scary part of that: our words set things in motion—positive or negative.

The Blueprint says, "And the tongue is a flame of fire. It is full of wickedness that can ruin your whole life. It can turn the entire course of your life into a blazing flame of destruction, for it is set on fire by hell itself" (James 3:6).

Ever regretted something you said and wished you could snatch the words back? But by then, things had been set in motion and there was nothing you could do about it. The events seemed to take on a life of their own and all you could do was watch in amazement or chagrin.

Do not take this for granted. The tongue is a catalyst of events, a creative force. You create what you say. The minute your words hit the atmosphere, a spiritual courier retrieves them to carry out what you have said—negative or positive. One of the most profound books I ever read was by Charles Capps, who wrote, many years ago, *The Tongue: A Creative Force*. It revolutionized my conversational and prayer life as I finally realized how much power words could have.

After all, remember that in the beginning there was nothing but the Word (Christ): "The Word was with God, and the Word *was* God"; "the Word became flesh" (John 1:1–2, 14 NIV). The Word created life. The Word created everything! God spoke and the earth and all of its inhabitants were formed by His Word. As His children, we have inherited the same creative ability to speak things into existence!

Words can build something wonderful or ruin a life. Words can come back to haunt us. This is why Paul said in the Architect's Blueprint, "You ought to be quiet and do nothing rashly" (Acts 19:36

NKJV). He recommended "that you also aspire to lead a quiet life, to mind your own business, and to work with your own hands" (1 Thess. 4:11 NKJV). You must apply effort—lots of it, sometimes—not to respond in the moment, no matter how passionate or justified you feel. What you don't say can be just as important as what you do say—remember that.

How you say what you say can be most critical of all. "[Speak] the truth in love," not in judgment, harshness, or manipulation (Eph. 4:15 NASB). If someone resists what we say because of our manner or our motives, no one will benefit even if what we said was correct and beneficial. Have a pure motive when you speak. Paul also suggested that we "lead a quiet and peaceable life in all godliness and reverence" (1 Tim. 2:2 NKJV). Peter the apostle said that a "gentle and quiet spirit [is] very precious in the sight of God" (1 Pet. 3:4 NKJV). Expensive things are rare things. Few can control their tongues, but control of your tongue is a powerful tool that will work for you.

Physical Habits

How you care for or use your body has long-term effects on your life—or can cut it short. Again, we have dominion over our bodies, they do not have dominion over us. Many await the generational maladies of their family lineage, never stopping to think that every family member who got diabetes or another malady ate the same way or had the same habits. Some who have realized this have taken control of their lives by changing their diets and being proactive about maintaining good health—and they have defied the odds, ending the cycle of bad health in their family line. (Granted, we can't avoid *all* those ills that "run in the family"—but we should do what we can.)

Lack of exercise and self-discipline has had repercussions on countless people. Abusing the body with extremes of activity has done just as much damage. We must remember to have a balanced approach to taking care of our bodies. Resilient *and* fragile, our bodies must be treated with respect. After all we each get only one...although, thanks to science, some parts can be replaced!

The Blueprint tells us the body is a temple and must be treated with reverence for what it carries—which is the Spirit of God Himself. You don't take precious cargo just anywhere, you take it only where others recognize its value. You don't submit it to abuse; no, you shelter and keep it safe.

You can tell by looking at some people they've lived hard lives. You can always see the results when people abuse their bodies with rough living, substance abuse, lack of rest and exercise, and all the wrong foods. It shows—big-time.

Except for the unforeseen occurrences in your future, the appearance of your body and the longevity of your life are, for the most part, up to you. The way you choose to maintain and sustain your body will affect your health and the length of your days. The Manufacturer will not circumvent poor maintenance on your part for the body He has left in your charge. So feed your body the right things, things that fuel your well-being and renew you when you're tired.

⁕

THOUGH YOU MAY be tempted to blame others for your habits, this is not permissible: this tool is entirely within your control. The habits you use to build your life will become as natural to you as breathing. The bottom line is *how you are and how you act* will dictate whether your life works—or doesn't.

CONSTRUCTION TIP

Your habits will drive all external responses and internal pressures in your life. As long as you remember that you are ultimately in control of this tool, you will be able to wield it appropriately and make the most of your life. The long and short of it: all of your habits are optional.

Character

H ave you ever met someone who looked good on paper but, when you got to know him, you found he was inconsistent, unreliable, and dishonest? It ruined whatever polished exterior he had presented to you. You could no longer vouch for that person because, to be perfectly honest, you could end up being guilty of his sin by association. No one wants to be associated with those who have bad character.

Good character is yet another tool that you can use to build or destroy a life. It affects every area: your personal relationships, your business interactions, your finances, your relationship with God—everything! Perhaps this is why the Master Architect spends so much time working on this one area of His design. He knows that if character is not developed properly, it will become a tool of destruction in the hand of His creation that will damage every part of life.

Your character is a tool that will work for you or against you. How, you say? Simply put, your character will form your reputation. Your reputation can affect your career as well as your personal relationships, intimate and otherwise, as you create a comfort level or a *discomfort* level for those you interact with.

Can you be trusted? Do you keep your word? Do you practice what you preach? People do not like uncertainty, and they do not like hypocrites. The fastest way to lose a job or wreck a relationship is to violate the trust of the one you are supposed to be serving or committed to.

King Solomon said, "A good reputation is more valuable than the most expensive perfume" (Eccl. 7:1). Now why would he compare a reputation to perfume? Because expensive perfume lingers in the air long after you're gone. It can be a welcome smell pleasing to the senses, or an offense that is a total turnoff to all who are assaulted by it. Your reputation is affecting your life even when you are not present. Your works and your words linger in the air and are discussed and dissected long after you've left the room. Unfortunately, first impressions can be lasting ones.

I once caught an assistant in the middle of a lie. After that I found myself questioning and double-checking everything she did. At times I felt guilty about my suspicions, but in the end, my fears were fully realized. My only mistake was not dealing with the issue of dishonesty sooner, before it cost me. Others warned me, but I didn't want to be "critical."

Someone once said if a person will lie, he will also steal. This takes us back to the tool of habits—these establish our character. The things that go unchecked in our lives become patterns of behavior—our "norm." The habitual liar actually believes his own lies! When you believe something you also justify it. Once you justify something, it's hard to believe that you should change it, even if it is ruining your life. Do the words, "Well, that's just the way I am" sound familiar?

Where Good Character Comes From

So how does one develop good character? Some are fortunate enough to learn early in life to make sound, wise choices. Sometimes, though, these people don't offer much grace for other people's failings because they can't relate to anything other than their own experiences. Other people are molded by experiencing the consequences of their words, choices, and actions. Hopefully they live to tell the story and exhibit the graciousness that can eventually come from lessons learned the hard way.

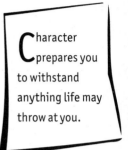

Character prepares you to withstand anything life may throw at you.

Though the Master Architect and Creator loves His creation, He understands the value of trials in perfecting character. The cedars of Lebanon become some of the hardest wood in the world because they are tested by the strong winds, broken and reinforced by the resin that is released from those breaks. Like those trees, we become strong people if we allow harsh experiences to make and not break us.

The Blueprint makes clear that it is through enduring and overcoming the hardships of life that you develop character, and character prepares you to withstand anything life may throw at you. The apostle James wrote: "Whenever trouble comes your way, let it be an opportunity for joy. For when your faith is tested, your endurance has a chance to grow. So let it grow, for when your endurance is fully developed, you will be strong in character and ready for anything" (James 1:2–4).

As you move forward in life, you should see a major fortification taking place in the core of your being: a strengthening, a tightening. No longer should your emotions be out of control, swinging to extremes every time something threatens to rock your world. Experience should saturate your mind-set, making you more sound and certain. There should be a consistency and even keel to your faith and responses in any given situation because you've weathered storms before and come through.

What Happens When You Use the Character Tool

When you practice good character, you face challenges in a steadfast and responsible way, not shirking your duties. You focus on what can be done and leave the rest to God, without considering that a sign of failure. You gracefully accept when it is time to face the music or simply let go.

If you have developed good character, you will own the consequences of your actions. You will not yield to condemnation, but you will respond to conviction and correction. A person with good character readily accepts wisdom and treats it as a friend. You do not celebrate foolishness or make excuses for or reward bad behavior. You set a standard that causes others to check themselves and either quietly align themselves with you or completely disengage.

The Key to a Life That Works

Why is the Creator so interested in your character? Because it is the secret to the life you want to live, that's why. And obviously since you are a reflection of Him and His glory, He wants you to live your best life. Character is your calling card, your entrée to the good life. Character flaws can interrupt your good fortune and make your life difficult, if not miserable.

Your character is the only reference people have to who you are. When you apply for a job, the company wants character references. We list people who will give us a favorable review. But what if someone hasn't had such a pleasant experience working with us, or we did not perform well on the job? How do we feel about having a potential employer get feedback from those former supervisors? We know that a negative review could cost us the job we want.

The same is true with relationships. When we're introduced to someone new, a potential love interest or friend, we know our character goes before us. What others say about us will influence this person, and what others say about him will influence our decision to get closer or move away.

Your character is such a powerful tool! It will speak for you louder than words or intentions. The consistent performance of wisdom, discretion, and integrity will vouch for you and bring you into the company of those who will champion you toward the life you truly want to live—a life that works.

All you have when you have completed your life is the reputation you leave behind. It will remain as a testament not only of who you were, but of who others became because of you. Good character causes you, as well as those around you to perform at your best and that truly makes life work for you and everyone else involved.

CONSTRUCTION TIP
A character is not someone you
pretend to be, it is who you are.

Assembly

❄ Open and Examine

❄ Own It

❄ Inspect the Building Site

❄ Get It Together

How to Assemble a Life That Works

Much depends on how you choose to put your life together. "To be or not to be?" is not the question here. Are you the best you can be? *This* is the question. How do you make that happen?

Let's look at a simple analogy: at a meal, every dish you serve has the potential to be a fabulous success or a terrible disaster depending on whether you follow the recipe and use the correct ingredients in the correct order and measure. It's one thing to know what goes into the dish but quite another to pull off the recipe to satisfaction. Such is life! It looks easy enough, but when you begin to line up all the parts, it can be quite a delicate dance to put them in the right order to get the great outcome you desire.

Some joke about their lives, "I've got to get my act together and take it on the road!" But life is not an act. There is nothing make-believe about it. When we are in the trenches of crisis, disappointment, or everyday grunt work, we experience life's deepest reality. Yet, despite our circumstances, it is totally up to us to get it together and keep it together with a little help from significant others and a whole lot of help from God.

In this section, let's take some time to consider how to assemble a life that works. Fools rush in, but wise men stop to consider the cost (Luke 14:28). After all, how you start is only half of it; how you finish is the sum total of your life. It pays to assess your design and the Architect's Blueprint, plan carefully, pace yourself, proceed wisely, and finish well.

After this life on Earth, another life awaits us. We are continually preparing for the future; therefore, we should build our lives carefully. Don't take the assembly process lightly. Now that you've established a foundation, secured your pillars, and gathered your tools, it's time to put your life together!

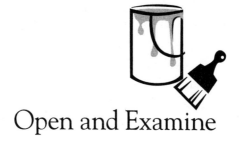

Open and Examine

Once you have a foundation, support structures, and tools, you have to take further steps to actually assemble a building. Open and examine are two of the first steps.

Open

Be Open with God

You must first be honest to the core with your Maker and Designer. God is not only the One who can guide you best through every maneuver of life, but He will also help you keep free and clear of any hindrance to living life well. When ravenous termites attack, He'll alert you. When a crack appears in your foundation, He'll make sure you notice in time to fix it as well as instruct you on how. He'll draw your attention to it immediately so no walls collapse. If what you've been building begins to implode, He will lift a standard against the destruction.

As the Master Architect, He is devoted to building something that lasts, something that shows His glory and handiwork. So He will be vigilant in keeping it sturdy and standing.

Remember Adam and Eve in the Garden of Eden? They first appear in the Manufacturer's Blueprint in Genesis 2. As long as they remained obedient, they were "naked...and were not ashamed" before God and one another and life was working for them (Gen. 2:25 NKJV). The garden they lived in was flourishing, every plant and animal was fruitful, and their relationship was peaceful and sublime.

But the moment they took life into their own hands, claiming their independence and eating the one fruit they had been warned against, their perfect life came to a screeching halt. The first thing they did was cover themselves: "Then the eyes of both of them were opened, and they knew that they were naked; and they sewed fig leaves together and made themselves coverings" (Gen. 3:7 NKJV).

I would dare to say, however, that they tried to cover themselves with more than fig leaves. I believe that their communication was also affected that day and they were unable to be as open with one another as they had been. We see deception slithering into the lives of the first couple, and then in all human beings after that.

After partaking of their snack, Adam and Eve were not only ashamed of themselves and embarrassed before one another, they also were afraid to face God. Though they had always looked forward to engaging in joyous, intimate fellowship with their Maker, now they ran to hide from Him. When discovered, instead of telling the truth about what they had done, Adam and Even both made sad excuses and beat around the bush (pardon the pun). And the punishment was loss of the perfect life they once knew.

Now man would work by the sweat of his brow and the woman would struggle in her relationship with the man, as well as suffer in childbearing. Listen to God's words:

He told the Woman:
"I'll multiply your pains in childbirth;
    you'll give birth to your babies in pain.
You'll want to please your husband,
    but he'll lord it over you."

He told the Man:

 "Because you listened to your wife
   and ate from the tree
 That I commanded you not to eat from
   'Don't eat from this tree,'
 The very ground is cursed because of you;
   getting food from the ground
 Will be as painful as having babies is for your wife;
   you'll be working in pain all your life long.
 The ground will sprout thorns and weeds,
   you'll get your food the hard way,
 Planting and tilling and harvesting,
   sweating in the fields from dawn to dusk,
 Until you return to that ground yourself, dead and buried;
   you started out as dirt, you'll end up dirt."

          (Genesis 3:16–19 *The Message*)

Though God graciously made a sacrifice on their account and covered them, He also ushered Adam and Eve from *Eden*, which means "pleasure." The pleasure of life was then distorted. Activities and relationships would no longer be as easy and effortless as they once were.

Though this is an extreme example, it illustrates just how vital it is to be open with God.

He did not come to the garden to accuse them of wrongdoing that day. And though He knew what they had done, He lovingly gave them the chance to come clean with Him. He does the same for us.

Be Accountable to Others

Two aspects of being open, transparency and accountability, are major assets that will keep you on track in life.

If you are the only person you are accountable to, you won't get far in life. Self-accountability becomes a breeding ground for excuses

When we retreat to our corners and begin to keep secrets, it is always a sign that something is not right.

that will assist you only in getting nothing done. In order to be accountable, you must be willing to be transparent: painfully honest, truthful about where you really are. This means you must do everything you can to make sure your life is free of pride or shame—two "termites" that can cause a lot of damage and can stop life from working as it should.

A lack of openness, of transparency and accountability, will always lead to a dissatisfying counterfeit of what our relationships as well as our lives are supposed to look—and work—like. (We see this glaring truth in Adam and Eve's story.)

When we refuse to be open, we set ourselves up to be deceived as well as deceptive. This is why the Architect is always testing us—to show us what is in our own hearts (Deut. 8:2). He knows the importance of allowing no pockets of darkness to accumulate in our spirits. When we retreat to our corners and begin to keep secrets, it is always a sign that something is not right.

The Blueprint says, "Men loved darkness rather than light, because their deeds were evil" (John 3:19 NKJV). This is why when "the Lord comes, he will bring our deepest secrets to light and will reveal our private motives" (1 Cor. 4:5). So why not keep life simple? Be open before you are opened! Choosing transparency will be far less painful than involuntary exposure.

Be Open to Change
Sometimes when God is ready to do a new thing in our lives, circumstances can get very uncomfortable first. This prepares us to be open to accepting something new. God is always moving forward. He

is progressive. Just when you think you're satisfied with the building you've built, He is ready to add on an addition or redecorate. He says, "See, I am doing a new thing! Now it springs up; do you not perceive it? I am making a way in the desert and streams in the wasteland" (Isa. 43:19 NIV). We are creatures of habit; we can sometimes dig in our heels even though we long for change in our hearts. In order for life to truly work, you have to be open to change.

Be Open to Life

Finally, be open to the endless possibilities of life. Dare to dream and envision the life you really want for yourself—choose to believe that it is possible. As you choose to believe that the same One who created and crafted you is able to make all the other pieces of your life fit together, choose to partner with Him (Mark 10:27). Then be open to His instruction. After all, He is the Creator of life. Who better to tell you how to make it work?

Examine

The second step in assembly is to examine yourself—with the help of your Creator. This is different from the self-examination in the You Cornerstone section. What I'm referring to here is a sort of integrity checkup. This may be hard because you will not always like what you see—which, of course, does not trouble the Master Architect of your life. He is already aware of your flaws and ready to assist you in transforming anything unsightly into a thing of beauty.

> "Come now, let us reason together,"
> Says the LORD,
> "Though your sins are like scarlet,

They shall be as white as snow;
Though they are red like crimson,
They shall be as wool." (Isaiah 1:18 NKJV)

God is able to make a glorious exchange: our pain and failure for His beauty, gladness, and praise. The prophet Jeremiah wrote:

GOD sent me to announce the year of his grace—
            a celebration of God's destruction of our enemies—
and to comfort all who mourn,
        To care for the needs of all who mourn in Zion,
give them bouquets of roses instead of ashes,
        Messages of joy instead of news of doom,
a praising heart instead of a languid spirit.
                                (Isaiah 61:2–3 *The Message*)

No matter what your inner struggle is, He is able to do an extreme makeover in your soul that will transform your life!

God, however, is a gentleman—He will not force you to undergo scrutiny. You must choose to let Him guide you as you probe your choices and attitudes and be open to what He may reveal. To willingly submit to the examination of the Lord makes way for you to be blessed: "I, the LORD, search all hearts and examine secret motives. I give all people their due rewards, according to what their actions deserve" (Jer. 17:10).

Enlist Tech Support, the Holy Spirit, to help you because the Spirit searches all things (1 Cor. 2:10). Not only will He show you the areas where improvement is needed but He will place a direct call to the Manufacturer on your behalf and order the needed parts to assist you. This is the greatest and most effective customer service you will ever experience!

The Holy Spirit helps us in our distress. For we don't even know what we should pray for, nor how we should pray. But the Holy Spirit prays for us with groanings that cannot be expressed in words. And the Father who knows all hearts knows what the Spirit is saying, for the Spirit pleads for us believers in harmony with God's own will. (Romans 8:26–27)

Who better to mediate for you than One who has connections with the Architect Himself?

Having the courage to face your flaws is empowering. To know yourself is the first step to building the life you want. When you know yourself inside and out, you will be able to mark out a clear strategy for moving forward. Integrity checkups equip you to know what things could interrupt your progress, so you'll be ready for them. This is called *living on the offense rather than on the defense*, which is rushing to put out fires as they occur. You will rarely be blindsided if you know what your spiritual and moral weaknesses are and can set healthy boundaries in place to compensate for them.

Ask yourself the following questions (I'll tell you in the next chapter what to do with what you find):

- How do I handle pressure? What is my first reaction? How has this hurt me in the past?
- How do I handle anger? What has been the result of my responses? What response do I really want? What do I need to do to get that response?
- What mistakes in my life continue to repeat themselves? What are the common denominators in all these repeat situations? What can I change?
- What are my weaknesses? What are my strengths? How can I make my strengths work for me and overpower my weaknesses?

❋ What are my areas of temptation? What realistic boundaries can I set to protect myself from falling? What mind-sets do I need to change?

You Can't Fix What You Don't Know About

Consider the benefits rather than fearing what your new self-knowledge will reveal. Don't be afraid to pray as King David did: "Search me, O God, and know my heart; test me and know my thoughts. Point out anything in me that offends you, and lead me along the path of everlasting life" (Ps. 139:23–24).

Remember, you cannot fix what you are unaware of. It is definitely easier to fix something when it is a little thing. Once it becomes a big problem, repair becomes a more costly venture—that is, if you are not beyond restoration.

A good example is my experience with my car. A "check engine" light came on in my car. After a while I took the car to the shop, where I learned that because I had waited so long to deal with the problem, other parts of the car were affected. Of course, the price of repair then became astronomical. Not only did the thermostat have to be replaced, so did the water pump and the timing belt and...As the list grew and I saw my budget going to the wind, I asked what we had to fix immediately and what could wait. I then received another list of instructions about when I would need to stabilize my car along with a warning that if I didn't attend to these things in a timely manner, many other things could go wrong. In short, I would need a new car! One little thing caused major problems that affected the life of my automobile. And so it is with life.

I saw a couple learn this the hard way in their relationship. The man was lost inside himself and quite moody and difficult. He dished out a lot of verbal abuse, and the woman took it silently because she really did love the man. Eventually the breaking point came: she cut off the relationship, much to the shock of the man, who had no idea he had been doing anything wrong. After all, she never told him that anything he did disturbed her!

After a lot of prodding on his part, she finally aired her grievances and the man was truly repentant. He just hadn't realized how much his words and actions had affected and offended her. He was more than remorseful and sought to mend his ways, but by then her love bank was depleted and she had nothing left to give. The relationship died.

In the final analysis, I have to say the responsibility for the demise of the relationship belonged to both of them: to him for behaving the way he did and to her for not saying anything sooner. Neither acted with true integrity. Examining yourself is not just about looking for your strengths and weaknesses—it is also about discerning your needs so that you can honestly share them with others in a healthy fashion. Relationships cannot thrive without communication and transparency.

The power to make life work comes from: (1) being known fully by our Creator, the Master Architect, God; (2) knowing ourselves so that we can set healthy standards for ourselves and healthy boundaries for those we interact with; (3) allowing ourselves to be known by others who add richness to our lives. Remember, you can own only what you acknowledge, and in order to acknowledge something you must discover it. That is when the adventure of life begins. And that is how life begins to work!

CONSTRUCTION TIP

If you'll take the steps of being open and conducting self-examination in cooperation with the Master Architect, passing inspection will ensure a great quality of life—one that will work without costly problems down the road.

Own It

That's right, you heard it here: now that you've been open and examined yourself with Tech Support's masterly guidance, it's time to own your stuff. Celebrate the good things you found and decide what you are going to do with the bad.

Hint: don't throw anything away without looking at it carefully, as nothing is ever really wasted when you're trying to put a life together. Your mistakes and failings can be your greatest teachers if you accept their lessons.

For example, anger can actually be good if it is refocused into passion that can be used for good. Many people have endured great tragedy and loss and used it to help others. One man, John Walsh, who lost his son to a murderer, went on to start *America's Most Wanted*, which is responsible for bringing many criminals to justice. Then there's the mother who founded MADD after her child was killed by a drunk driver. Perhaps your experience is not as dramatic; perhaps it was a heartbreak, or a job-related experience. Whatever it is, flip the script on it, learn from it, and use it for good. Let it bring the best out of you and not the worst.

It's All Yours

Again, your life belongs to you. No one can make you do anything to make your life work or cause it to fail. That decision, my friend, is entirely up to you.

So claim your life, embrace it, look at it objectively and realistically, and own every single part of it. Up to now the choices you've made, the people you've embraced, the ideas you've accepted, the beliefs you've ascribed to all belong to you. Somewhere along the way you integrated them into the delicate design of your life. These interactions became conclusions that solidified who you are.

I've heard adults blame the outcome of their lives on their parents, people who said something negative to them, a traumatic experience, a relationship gone sour. I shake my head and wonder why they are allowing temporary, external contributors to have so much power over their lives. After all, they are now adults! They can do or say whatever they want. They no longer have to be ruled by things they couldn't control in the past. Yet many choose to be victims instead of victors. Dare I add—many became volunteers who signed up for misery.

To become a victor, admittedly, requires work. As long as you won't own your stuff, you won't be able to change anything. This is why we need to enlist the help of the Holy Spirit (more on this in the Tech Support section). The Holy Spirit is the conveyer of truth, but He is also a counselor. He will reveal the intimate details of the Master Architect's divine Blueprint for your life. He will help you change those spiritual and moral failings.

Listen Up

The Spirit can't do you any good if you don't pay attention to what He shows you. In other words:

> Do not merely listen to the word, and so deceive yourselves. Do what it says. Anyone who listens to the word but does not do what it says is like a man who looks at his face in a mirror and, after looking at himself, goes away and immediately forgets what he looks like. [Talk about being in denial!] But the man who looks intently into the perfect law that gives freedom, and continues to do this, not forgetting what he has heard, but doing it—he will be blessed in what he does. (James 1:22–25 NIV)

Should I be even more direct? "Fools despise wisdom and discipline" (Prov. 1:7 NIV). The flip side of that is: "He who gets wisdom loves his own soul; he who cherishes understanding prospers" (Prov. 18:9 NIV).

Keep It Real

You have to know you need direction in order to receive it, which means you have to be willing to admit your weaknesses, shortcomings, and failures. This is an exercise not in beating yourself up but in keeping it real. As I've said before, life does not just happen. Work is involved. Strategy is involved. Disciplines are involved. Systems must be put in place. It's like a business.

Yes, your life is your business. You are the president and CEO. The board can have its opinions, but the final word is up to you. The only other opinion that matters is God's, because He has invested more into your life than you have, and yet He graciously lets you have the final say though He could actually be the controlling partner!

Every CEO with a growing business constantly examines its productivity, its employees, its systems to look for ways to heighten efficiency and profitability. The examination never stops; each milestone reached offers valuable information about what worked or what bogged down the system. A successful CEO revisits how his company works time and time again.

So now that you've taken stock, own your stuff. Don't blame someone else for your troubles. Again, we decide what we allow or disallow. This is why the Blueprint instructs us that whatever we loose in Earth is loosed in heaven, and whatever we bind on Earth is bound in heaven (Matt. 18:18). This means the forces of heaven pay attention to every decision you make. They either help support your godly choices or move aside to avoid the fallout of your ungodly ones. We have been given authority over our lives.

Don't Wimp Out

Owning your stuff means you do whatever it takes to overcome on all levels, naturally and spiritually. We've already talked about spiritual warfare. Remember Elijah, the weary and depressed prophet (1 Kings 17, 18)? God revealed to him that, contrary to his beliefs, he was not alone in his struggles. God gave Elijah time to recover physically and emotionally but never let him off the hook. Life went on and he had to finish his course.

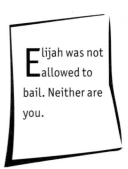
Elijah was not allowed to bail. Neither are you.

Elijah was not allowed to bail. Neither are you.

As you own your stuff and sort it all out, you'll be better equipped to assemble a life that works.

CONSTRUCTION TIP
You will always lose if you choose to play the blame game.
Those who grasp life firmly, owning all their choices,
gain from their experiences and eventually win.

Inspect the Building Site

Geography has a lot to do with how your life will work. No doubt you've heard the rule of thumb for real estate purchases: "Location, location, location!" Where you put your life will have a lot to do with how well it works.

Geography has everything to do with whether you thrive in life. Certain plants and trees must be planted in certain types of soil and climate in order to grow and bear fruit. When planted in the wrong place, they die. Sometimes where you start is not the place most conducive to finishing what you've begun. The Israelites were welcome in Egypt and revered because of Joseph, but years later, after Joseph had died and a new Pharaoh rose up, the once-welcoming Egyptians enslaved the Israelites. The place of refuge and sustenance became a place of bondage.

Sometimes we linger in the same place or situation way too long—the wrong locale, the wrong job, the wrong relationship....We find our walls looking worse for wear and our pillars shaky. The roof is developing numerous leaks and the chimney is plugged. You have to be sensitive to the climate and environment you are in. If you are someplace where you can't

> Where you put your life will have a lot to do with how well it works.

seem to build a fulfilling life, it may be time to seek new, more encouraging surroundings. If, for example, you're trying to be a big-time actor, Idaho is probably not the place for you; try New York or California.

Stay Put Till You Know It's Time to Move

Before you take a step, you should know what you are stepping into. Many years ago, after losing my job in Chicago, I decided to move to Los Angeles. Totally unaware of my gifts or what I had to offer, I was unable to find a job in my field, which was advertising and graphic design. I ended up working temporarily at many jobs that were not fulfilling or even enjoyable. I floundered.

I was finally called back to Chicago, to my original job in advertising. Upon my return, I received a massive raise and new doors of opportunity were opened to me. I also ended up singing and doing voice-overs on the commercials I wrote and discovered more of my gifts. I could have used all the things I discovered about myself in LA, but I did not have a handle on those gifts yet. Therefore I failed to be fruitful when I tried a new location. Many have said, "If I knew then what I know now, what a different life I would have led." But would you have led a God-designed life? That is the question. How much we leave to the divine and how much we take hold of and control is a delicate balance. Sometimes God does not reveal certain things to us because He knows we would hurt ourselves with information. Sometimes He keeps us where we are because we are not ready for that job or another city. Here again, consulting with the Master Architect and His Blueprint is essential.

It is crucial that we continually seek Him and follow His instruction. When He gives none, wait for the next cue. Meanwhile, continue to nurture and develop the gifts and skills you know you have in the setting He has assigned you. Maintain your present course until you receive further notice to change direction. Do it with a grateful heart until the next door opens. As much as possible, enjoy your current location until God opens up another.

Sometimes everything around you has to dry up, thus forcing you to move when a clear directive or new opportunity presents itself. However, never move without being sure you are making a God move and not just a good move! A life created without consulting the Architect or His Blueprint is a life that just won't work.

CONSTRUCTION TIP
Being in the right place at the right time is everything
to constructing a life that works. For proof,
check out the Blueprint!

Get It Together

How you put everything in your life together is just as important as the parts you use and the elements you construct. The Master Architect is a God of order and, in His divine Blueprint, there is a prescribed order to life. When we get out of spiritual order, chaos ensues.

As you consider the parts we've discussed in the order we discussed, you should see a pattern emerging. A stable and beautiful life is built around God. Its floors are solid, weathered and finished by lessons learned over time. Its walls are covered by grace, and the light of truth illuminates every window and casts a liberating glow on every facet of your life. All is kept intact and covered by the salvation of the Master Architect. Within this durable structure He has left lots of room for you to make your own additions, renovations, and interior design decisions.

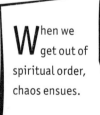

When we get out of spiritual order, chaos ensues.

As you move forward to the Maintenance part of this guide, know and understand that additions, renovations, and decorations are optional, but the main parts and order of construction are not. The maintenance components are the things that will seal, insulate, and keep all that you invest in your life in mint condition. Having a realistic approach to your life will let you know just how much is needed to balance your life and make it work for you.

The goal is to build a life that will not fall apart under pressure, get easily shaken, collapse from the damage of stress, or be moved by outside elements. Your life should not only work for you, it should be a beacon of hope and an oasis for others. It should stand strong, reflecting the mastery and divine design of the Master Architect.

Like the buildings tourists rush to see, your life should be an attraction, a landmark with a rich history of wonderful achievements and a testimony of a life well lived. These types of buildings take time to create as well as great attention to detail. So as you build, decide to build carefully and be willing to do what's required to preserve everything that has been put in place, while always leaving room for more.

Maintenance

Preventative

- ☀ Prayer
- ☀ Sound Counsel
- ☀ Understanding
- ☀ Discretion
- ☀ Diligence
- ☀ Insight
- ☀ Diet
- ☀ Rest
- ☀ Balance

Long-Term

- ☀ Self-Control
- ☀ Perseverance
- ☀ Godliness
- ☀ Love
- ☀ Consistent Growth

Make It Look Good (and Work, Too)

I t's one thing to build a life, it's another to maintain it and keep it functioning. Look at the state of the lives around you. Depending on your circle of friends, your view could range from a high-end, highly manicured–looking block to a run-down ghetto. Some lives have been wisely and solidly constructed and show no signs of abuse, only the refinement that comes from age and wearing well. Others look worse for wear with surface abrasions and cracks in the foundation that have moved up the walls and threaten to topple the entire structure. If you venture deeper into these interiors, you'll find some beams shaky, boards falling apart, leaky pipes, rusted nails, and general debris building up. Some houses may be in such poor repair they appear to have been abandoned.

It's true that some lives, like houses, appear to have been kept up but inside they are falling to pieces. Both inside and outside need upkeep so they can bear the burdens of life without overtaxing one or the other.

This requires great ongoing care. You can put some preventative measures in place that will keep you from subjecting your life to undue stress. You need to also practice long-term maintenance that will ensure not only a good life but a lasting one. In this section we will examine ways to help you run life as smoothly as possible.

Never fall prey to the myth that life should be easy or problem-free. Even the Master Architect warned you ahead of time: "In this world you will have trouble. But take heart! I have overcome the world" (John 16:33 NIV). He goes on to reassure us, "Everyone who has been born of God overcomes the world" (1 John 5:4 ESV). The question is not *if* the elements will assault your life, the question is simply *when*—and will you be prepared to stand and weather changing conditions (pun intended). Sometimes it is impossible to dance between the raindrops of life; therefore, you have to be prepared to stand no matter what, knowing that the rain and the tears will dry and life will go on in spite of it all.

The condition of your life, as you experience the common difficulties, will be up to you. In the end it's the flaws and watermarks that make us all interesting. So let's dig into planning our work and working our plan. A key to maintaining a life that works is having a working maintenance plan. These are the things that you *can* control, the things that will keep your life running no matter what.

Preventative Maintenance: Prayer

I f you think you can get through this life without prayer, you are sadly mistaken. You can fake it, but when life hits the fan the only lifeline that will get you through is prayer. There is a reason the Master Architect mandates that "men ought always to pray, and not to faint" (Luke 18:1 KJV). Notice the link. Prayer is the thing that enables you not to give up, not to give in to stress and fear, not to abdicate your authority over the events in your life.

On that note let's understand what prayer is, what it does, how to do it effectively, and why it needs to be a habit in your life. Lest you get it twisted, prayer is not a monologue. It is a two-way conversation between you and your Master Creator—God—the One who knows and loves you most, the One who also has a bird's-eye view of all concerning you. You talk to Him. You shut up and wait. He talks to you. When we choose to make prayer a habit daily, continually, the results of that quality conversation time truly manifest themselves in every area of our lives.

People always say that prayer changes things, but I believe the most effective prayer changes *you*. When you change, your circumstances change as everyone and everything surrounding you has to line up with the new you. A different attitude calls for different actions, which lead to different results. When you take the time to commune with the One who sees and knows all things, you will get quality instruction. Only then can you build a life that works *and* lasts.

Small wonder Jesus retreated early in the morning and again in the evening to have conversations with God. God is known to be "a revealer of secrets" (Dan. 2:47 NKJV)—the things you could not know because they are hidden from the human eye: the inside scoop on a spouse's heart, conversations about you at work, what your children are doing and not telling you, and more.

In order for the steps of the righteous to be "ordered" of God (Ps. 37:23 NKJV), you must report for duty. As a good soldier stands before the captain awaiting instruction, we must get instruction from the One who holds the Blueprint for our lives. It is only in the exchange of conversation that we can tap into the mind of Christ and begin to think as He does (1 Cor. 2:16). Only an intimate relationship can change our hearts and our mind-sets. This is why religion will always fail: going through the motions without the emotions that come from intimacy leaves room for us to become harsh, irrational, and loveless with others.

How Can We Know the Mind of the Maker?

By His Spirit
Exactly how does He communicate with us? First, by His Spirit to our spirits. As a matter of fact, He supplies such Tech Support even if you don't know how to pray! The Holy Spirit intercedes on your behalf in accordance with the will of the Father (Rom. 8:26–28). That deep sense of knowing you feel at your core is His Spirit communicating directly with your spirit.

By His Word
Second, we hear from God through His written Word, your Blueprint for life, the Bible. His instructions are very clear and, contrary to popu-

lar belief, He does not contradict Himself or change His mind about what He says. Many try to cross-examine God in prayer, asking the same question over and over again, hoping He will change His response. They then wonder why He remains silent. The answer to that is simple. He has already written what He had to say on the subject, and there is no need for Him to repeat Himself. Besides, His answer will never be different from the original. Perhaps it's time for you to change your question!

Some don't want to know what He has to say on a subject so they just don't ask. Let me assure you that ignorance will never be bliss because ignorance will never lead you to the life you are seeking.

By His People

Frequently God uses others in our lives to help us discern what is happening and what we should do (more on this in the next section). Notice in the Bible how God used prophets to warn kings and the disciples to help others find the way to heaven and solve everyday problems and issues.

By Circumstances

God also uses circumstances to direct us. This is why every closed door should be considered a detour as opposed to the end of the road. He gently directs us, that is, if we really want Him to. This is where we get the direction we need to make sound choices that work for our lives, our relationships, and everything else concerning us. This is why there is no excuse for not making progress in life. All we have to do is follow the instructions He so graciously gives in times of prayer and meditation on His Word.

Again, this does not mean we will be exempt from trouble, but it equips us to handle all that comes our way, understanding that the present trials of the day are simply preparation for the greatness that is to come. This is enduring the process of transformation, ever changing, growing greater and stronger according to the Creator's design.

When Is the Best Time to Pray?

Many insist that morning is absolutely the best time. They feel so strongly about it that they imply you are doomed if you don't practice what they preach. For those who are not morning people, this may pose a problem. I am a firm believer that how you begin your day will determine how the rest of it will go; therefore, it would be best to begin your day with a conversation with the One who can lay out a plan for you. To start the day without prayer is like setting off on a journey without looking at the map first. After driving for some time without reaching your destination, when you stop to consult your directions you find, to your dismay, that you have driven far from where you intended. This would not have happened if you had looked at the map first.

All of that said, many go through unnecessary pain, stress, and effort because they don't pray. Regardless of whether you are a morning, noon, or nighttime person, the reality of life as well as the Manufacturer's Blueprint require that you "pray without ceasing" (1 Thess. 5:17 NKJV).

Prayerfully consider every choice you make, every step you take, and even when the way grows hard you will be equipped with what you need to stand strong and not be carried away by life's dramas. You will have clarity and hope in spite of your circumstances because your connection to God is reinforced regularly. Prayer should be like breathing to you—natural and necessary. It does not need to be elaborate or loud. It is communion, sweet and simple—pouring out your heart in honesty, being direct and to the point.

> To start the day without prayer is like setting off on a journey without looking at the map first.

Prayer is for you more than it is for God. Even though He desires fellowship with us, let's face it: His life is not going to fall apart if we don't talk to Him, but ours will.

It Just Makes Sense

It simply makes sense to pray. If you knew you had access to the president of a company and didn't have to go through any of his support staff, wouldn't you take advantage of that option? God says to come to Him without the lengthy soliloquies: "Heathen...think that they will be heard for their many words" (Matt. 6:7 NKJV). Just spit it out! Humbly state your requests to Him (Phil. 4:6), and as you pray in the will of the Father He will grant your requests!

What does that mean? Don't go asking for stuff you know He is not going to agree with. That is the best way not to get your prayer answered. God will not be manipulated and will not do anything against His Word. Sometimes His silence is His lack of agreement as He waits for you to change your requests to something with which He is willing to cooperate. Selfish requests will not be answered. Praying based on personal lusts rather than a desire that would serve others besides yourself will find no answer (James 4:3).

Again, prayer is a two-sided conversation. Take the time to pour out your heart, concerns, and requests to God but then also take the time to still your mind and your spirit and listen. He will speak in the stillness and show you things that you know not of (Jer. 33:3)—the secrets you need to succeed with a long-lasting, well-working life!

CONSTRUCTION TIP
Without consistent consultation with the Master Architect, building the life you want will come to a standstill.

Preventative Maintenance: Sound Counsel

A man or a woman who walks alone for too long will only get lost. There is safety in surrounding yourself with a multitude of good advisors: "Plans go wrong for lack of advice; many counselors bring success" (Prov. 15:22). We've all experienced it: being in the car with someone (maybe even ourselves) who did not want to ask for directions when you both knew you were lost. As you drifted farther from your destination your frustration grew because you knew you were wasting gas and time. Nothing can be more maddening than watching someone make a mistake he or she really didn't have to.

The thing that usually stops people from seeking counsel is pride. But you know what they say about that—"Pride goes before destruction, and haughtiness before a fall" (Prov. 16:18). Life just does not work well without counsel. Everyone needs a sounding board and a voice of reason or direction. We were created for fellowship and sharing. We are called to exhort one another to good works. This means exchanging ideas and resources as well as lending knowledge and encouragement. No one functions well alone.

It is dangerous to become myopic in scope and see things only from your own point of view: if you insist on this, you are destined to miss something! Sound counsel provides the rearview and side mirrors in your life that will reveal what is hidden in your blind spots. Therefore, welcome counsel, listen, and consider—place on hold what does not resound with you, then keep and use the good stuff.

After all the voices have had their say, make sure the decisions you make concerning your life are grounded in peace. If you don't have a peace about something, *do not do it*. Listen to your internal alarm. It might be the wrong time; it might be the wrong action. So consider what others are saying, but let your peace level lead your timing as well as your choices. In the meantime, do what you can do until you feel a release to tackle the rest.

Good Counsel and Bad

Now, there is a difference between counsel and sound counsel. My mother once told me opinions are like noses—everyone has one. Everybody can give advice, but what do you keep and what do you throw away? You need the counsel that leads to life, not death, disappointment, and despair; the kind that energizes you and equips you to build whatever the Architect assigns. Without clear direction and the right information, the choices we make become a haphazard gamble where winning is not guaranteed and misery becomes a regular visitor. With the influx of life coaches, counselors, and information services for every area of life, there is no shortage of resources for receiving all types of counsel.

Sound counsel is crucial to every area of life. In areas ranging from finance to romance you will need objective parties to speak into your life offering clarity, solutions, and fresh perspective. No business moves forward or goes to the next level without consulting with experts on the issues of branding, positioning, and change management. A company will pay a fortune in consulting fees to make its goals a reality. Many couples who find their marriages in crisis seek counseling. Those who mutually cooperate and do the work it takes to make love work are able to salvage and advance their relationships. Those who do not... well, they usually go on to make the same mistakes in the next relationship.

Even God knows the importance of counsel. And because He knows no one greater than Himself, He counsels with Himself and consults with Wisdom. Wisdom in the personification of a woman in the book of Proverbs lets us know that she was the first work the Master Architect ever created and she was there, consulting with God at the creation, helping Him as He marked out the foundations of the earth (Prov. 8:22–30). Even God is aware that "plans succeed through good counsel" (Prov. 20:18). How much more do you need to seek wisdom through counsel beyond your own?

So Where Do You Get the Good Stuff?

Whom should you listen to? There's a lot of bad advice floating around out there, and so many self-help gurus. Don't get me wrong. Self-help material is bad only if the guru is armed with just his or her opinions. It's important to know where one's opinions come from. If they do not come from the Manufacturer's Blueprint, I don't care how good the secrets and suggestions sound—they are worthless.

Let me rephrase that. Self-help material needs not only to derive from the One who created counsel and wisdom, it needs to be repeated in the right context—not doctored up to suit any person's personal agenda and rationale (and bank account).

There are several places you can get the good stuff—the best counsel around.

1. God
Your first source of counsel should of course be God. He is always faithful to give sound and wise instruction. When left to our own

devices, we can end up in a heap of trouble. I think of Joshua, a mighty and fierce leader of Israel who got tricked into making an alliance with Israel's enemies simply because he listened to what the seemingly innocent strangers said, accepted their gifts, and "did not consult the LORD" (Josh. 9:14). Not a smart move. Once the vow was made, Joshua and the Israelites had to tolerate the Gibeonites rather than destroy them. These people became lifetime irritants—kind of like the lousy spouse you get in an unwise marriage or the debt you incur from a bad business partnership.

Consult with God about everything and follow His good advice. That's what wise people do.

2. Yourself

Counsel with yourself. Yes, that's right: listen to your inner voice. This is the voice of the Holy Spirit whispering the counsel of God to you. How often have you said, "Something told me to..."? That was not some*thing*, it was some*one*. Often we battle with this one: *Was that God or was that me?* It's a good question to ask since our hearts can so easily deceive us.

Yet counsel is simple to cross-check and confirm. For starters, just make sure any "nudge" or suggestion matches the instructions found in the Manufacturer's Blueprint. If the instructions you are receiving are contrary to the Word of God, you have not heard from God. Quick—cast down those imaginations! If, however, what you heard matches God's character and even biblical examples, move forward.

If you take a wrong turn, the Holy Spirit will be right there to wave a red flag. You will not feel settled or comfortable with your decision, which is your signal that something is not right. When in doubt or unrest, do nothing. Stop. Wait until you get a peace

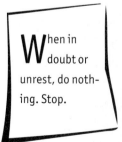

When in doubt or unrest, do nothing. Stop.

about what you are about to do or receive clarity on the issue. When you receive the release in your spirit that signals it's fine to move forward, do so.

3. Wise, Experienced People

Wise people know whom to listen to. This is one of my favorite excerpts from the Manufacturer's Blueprint.

> Oh, the joys of those
> > who do not follow the advice of the wicked,
> > or stand around with sinners,
> > or join in with scoffers.
> But they delight in doing everything the LORD wants;
> > day and night they think about his law.
> They are like trees planted along the riverbank,
> > bearing fruit each season without fail.
> Their leaves never wither,
> > and in all they do, they prosper. (Psalm 1:1–3)

That is the ultimate manifestation of a life that is flourishing: consistent production of good things, not just materially but relationally and spiritually; good things that last along with increasing prosperity. Isn't that what everyone wants?

How do you get that? By running with and taking counsel from the right people. (As a life-that-works principle, avoid, at all costs, those who have no respect for the Word of God or even for life itself. If you know some people like that, ask God whether they have been placed in your life so you can be a positive influence. If that is the case you should set the standard, not follow it. Otherwise move on to greener pastures with better sheep.)

When facing a big decision, if you hear a loud chorus of people you respect and love voicing caution, take another look before continuing. Your circle of friends should be a reliable source of counsel. As a matter of fact, their "heartfelt counsel" should be "as sweet as perfume and incense" (Prov. 27:9).

Experience, good or bad, can save you from shame. Yours and others' experiences should teach you what *not* to do just as much as they teach you what to do. Real-life experience is a priceless source of wisdom.

"Only fools despise wisdom and discipline" (Prov. 1:7). A wise man will listen and increase his knowledge base because he understands that the only way to have true understanding is to attain counsel. Look at what Solomon wrote at the beginning of Proverbs: "Let those who are wise listen to the proverbs and become even wiser. And let those who understand receive guidance by exploring the depth of meaning in these proverbs, parables, wise sayings, and riddles" (Prov. 1:5–6).

When choosing counselors, understand the importance of the source. There is a reason why some people's lives are not working; these are people you do not want to listen to.

Vital Timing and Complete Information

Wise people also know the importance of timing and not moving forward until they have enough information. The greatest killer of any great idea or plan can be a lack of information. Moving forward in ignorance is the quickest way to lose a war. You can have all the faith in the world but if you are not armed with the right information, you will make the wrong choices and lose everything—love, money, you name it!

Again, when in doubt, don't move; stand still and ask questions, lots of them, until you feel the release in your spirit to go forward. Counsel with God, commune with yourself, and seek information from wise, respected people of understanding. Look at what God told Moses to instruct His people: "Choose wise and discerning men from your tribes, and I will appoint them as your heads" (Deut. 1:13 NASB).

What information you accumulate and when you choose to act can save you, equip you, and promote you to the next level of living, loving, and overcoming. And that is what life looks like when everything is working.

CONSTRUCTION TIP
Make sure to seek sound counsel liberally. This will guard against impulse and foolish moves that can threaten everything you desire in a life that works.

Preventative Maintenance: Understanding

Everyone on the face of the earth longs to be understood. This is the gateway to connecting with others and having relationships that work not only in your personal life but also in business. Understanding is a rare and wonderful virtue to have. We've touched on this already, but let me confirm: comprehending the information you've been given is key to being able to effectively connect with anyone you encounter. Simply put, understanding is knowing what to do with the knowledge you attain.

In my research, I found that the Hebrew word for understanding is *manda*, which is translated as the "power of knowledge." True understanding is knowledge translated into an attitude that serves your best interests. It helps you to shun evil as well as foolishness and offense. You might wonder why I say that, so let's take a look at what understanding gets you.

Six Ways Understanding Helps

1. Understanding Opens Doors for You
First of all, understanding helps you to hold your tongue. It helps you to know when to speak and when to be silent. Having understanding

means you know that even when you are right, voicing your sentiment in the immediate moment might not be the wisest move;
you recognize the power of timing and grace in order to really be
heard.

This is huge! The word well placed can open up the world for you;
wrongly put, it can slam countless doors (Prov. 25:11). Words said
appropriately can set you apart in a room and make what you have to
say valuable to the listener. When people like you, they will respond
to you and open doors you could not imagine. Remember this: when
people don't like you, they won't help you, and when they don't help
you, it can hurt you.

In other words, understanding can gain tremendous favor for you:
"A person with good sense is respected" (Prov. 13:15).

2. Understanding Deepens Your Relationships

To be heard and understood is something everyone wants but not
everyone receives. I believe it is one of the things that made Jesus
so popular with those who were wounded and down-and-out. He
seemed to feel what they felt and it created a bond between them and
inspired them to follow His leadership.

If you want to be an effective leader, teacher, friend, spouse, parent,
or coworker, understand your employees, your students, your friends,
your mate, your children, and your colleagues. Know where they are
coming from and you will be able to give them effective instruction.
They will receive the instruction because they feel connected to
you. When you understand others, you make them feel significant—
something everyone longs for.

Everyone loves an understanding ear. People with understanding
get down in the trenches with people they are addressing and stand
under them in order to lift them up. If you have understanding, you
will be a servant to those you talk to.

3. Understanding Helps You Avoid Evil

As I mentioned, understanding can guard you, establish you, and keep you from evil: "Acquire wisdom! Acquire understanding!...Do not forsake her, and she will guard you" (Prov. 4:5–6 NASB).

Being told not to do something has never been enough for anyone. One of the first questions a child asks is "Why?" He or she wants to understand. People all over the world have questioned everything, from why certain things happen to why God says what He does and allows the things that take place in the world to happen. The struggle to understand is built into our nature, and God is fine with that. As a matter of fact, He says, "With all your getting, get understanding" (Prov. 4:7 NKJV).

Make it one of your chief pursuits to attain not only wisdom but understanding as well; it is this one thing that will help you keep all that you acquire. Understanding gives you peace with the instruction you receive. When God, a parent, or a friend speaks into your life, understanding he or she speaks from a heart that loves you and wants the best for you helps you to receive his or her instruction. Without that understanding, you may become defensive, rebellious, and self-destructive, choosing not to heed the instruction given for your own good. In the end you suffer and hear the words, "I told you so!"

4. Understanding Gives You Self-Discipline

Understanding will also give you self-discipline. I understand that if I keep sweets in my house, I will devour them all in one sitting; therefore, I don't keep sweets in the house. Watching my weight and health is important to me. How about you? If you understand what your actions will cost you, perhaps you won't be so quick to do things that are detrimental to your health, your relationships, or your finances. You will make wise and educated choices when you possess understanding; it will help you to keep a straight course and maintain order in your life. This is essential in order for you to prosper in every area of your life.

God is a God of order. The heavens are perfectly aligned. Plants blossom, wither, die, and spring back to life on a regular basis. We know when to expect the change of the seasons because God has set it in order. Without order, chaos reigns. No one gets anything done in the midst of disorder because it opens the door for everything to fall through the cracks, leaving nothing to show for all your hard work and energy.

5. Understanding Gives You Patience

Ultimately understanding gives you patience because when you understand some things—such as the value of perfect timing—you can wait for the outcome you want. You will be able to see not only the big picture of your situation but also the tiny details. You will be able to plot your course based on what you know and set reasonable and realistic time tables for advancing your mission.

Why do you think a year to us is as a thousand to the Lord (Ps. 90:4)? Why is He so long-suffering and patient with people in the world in spite of the horrendous things they sometimes do? Because He understands the frailty of humanity and what those weaknesses subject us to: fear, pride, brokenness, all sorts of things that can cause us to act and react in a wrong fashion. His understanding is one of the things that deepens His love for us and causes Him to extend grace to us.

6. Understanding Will Prosper You

This is the greatest reward of understanding: it will prosper you. For example, God's understanding of our weaknesses makes Him choose to wait until He can gather as many as possible to Himself before allowing the end of time. In the end His understanding will pay off and He will get what He wants—collectively the bride of Christ, many souls coming home to be with Him.

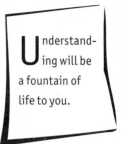

Understanding will be a fountain of life to you.

This is what understanding will do for you. It will help you flourish in every area of your life because you have a grasp on the whys, hows, and what fors. You will know when to act and when to wait. Understanding will be a fountain of life to you.

Where Can I Get Some?

Understanding comes from a healthy respect for God and knowledge of His Word. Although His ways are not our ways and He operates on a higher level of understanding, He loves mankind enough to share His thoughts through His Word. He says "Knowledge of the Holy One is understanding" (Prov. 9:10 NIV).

As you come to understand the heart of God, you will gain perspective on His commands and instruction. You also gain a better understanding of the nature of man and how the world operates. This will empower you to live above the little irritants that can impede your progress in life. When you comprehend His power, wisdom, and knowledge, you will respect His Word and follow His instructions.

If getting a personal understanding of God through the Word does not appeal to you, go ahead and learn the hard way. Live long enough and you will understand plenty. As the old folks say, "We'll all understand it by and by." Yes, long life will most definitely make you understand some things (Job 12:12). Give every event enough breathing space and you will have an "aha" moment if you choose to learn the lesson.

It's so much easier to seek understanding from the One who wrote life's Blueprint. From Him you can learn the lessons that are invaluable when it comes to making life work.

CONSTRUCTION TIP
Apply understanding to every area of your life. Though it can be expensive, it will be even more costly in the long run if you never acquire it.

Preventative Maintenance: Discretion

This is an attribute that has to be mastered. You need understanding and maturity in order to exercise it, but it will protect you (Prov. 2:11). Many a politician has been publicly shamed at the height of his career for indiscretions. A lack of judgment results in foolish actions that can cost a person everything. In most cases a moment of guilty pleasure turns into a perpetual nightmare. This is why you need to use discretion to maintain the good life you have built.

Moments of temptation come. Life-changing decisions are made in an instant, in a rush of emotion. The tyranny of the urgent will convince you that you need that thing, that opportunity, that man right now. Later you find your choice created more problems than it was worth—all for temporary gratification, a quick fix.

Choices made out of good judgment are what discretion is all about. Discretion is a wonderful quality you apply when treating others and their personal business with respect and confidentiality. To be known as a keeper of secrets is powerful in

Having discretion is using good judgment in tough situations.

relationships—it makes other people feel safe. Having discretion is using good judgment in tough situations.

Let's look at a few ways discretion helps maintain a well-built life.

Discretion Protects

Consider the plight of Joseph (Gen. 39). He was sold into slavery by his brothers, then purchased as a servant by an important citizen in Egypt. Though Joseph enjoyed his master's respect, his master's wife wanted to enjoy Joseph himself. When he faced the temptation of Mrs. Potiphar, who continually pursued him for an adulterous affair, he utilized discretion.

One could sympathize with Joseph, being lonely in a foreign land, estranged from friends and family, in need of comfort and solace. Why not respond to a woman who was throwing herself at him? Yet he took the time to make the right judgment call. He even tried to reason with her: "Look...my master trusts me with everything in his entire household. No one here has more authority than I do! He has held back nothing from me except you, because you are his wife. How could I ever do such a wicked thing? It would be a great sin against God" (Gen. 39:9).

Mrs. Potiphar ignored Joseph's response and continued her "come hither" moves. In the end she was embittered and falsely accused him of rape. This might cause one to wonder, *What is the reward for making the right choice?* But Joseph's righteous choice prevailed by putting him in the right position to rise to power later.

I wonder how Mrs. Potiphar felt the day she got the news that Joseph had been promoted to right-hand man of the Pharaoh. Did she quake in terror at the prospect of his seeking retribution for her false accusations? Sometimes I think the juiciest parts of the story are omitted from Scripture—however, we are given what we need to know. What we especially need to know from this scenario is that discretion protected Joseph.

The right choice will always be the right choice because truth will always prevail. Good will always overpower evil. A wrong choice will always be a wrong choice even if the results of that choice don't manifest until long after the initial act. Make no mistake—bad choices will always catch up with you.

They certainly caught up with Samson (Judg. 14–16). Wrong woman after wrong woman finally led to his demise. Driven by his flesh and anger, he succumbed to three powerful forces—his desires, his temper, and the seduction of a woman. He had to be blinded in order to see the error of his ways and what it finally cost him—death way too soon in a young and promising life.

Discretion Cleans Up Your Conversation

You should exercise discretion not just with your actions but with your attitude and words. There is nothing worse than a conversation run amuck—someone out of control, talking too much, giving too much information (or TMI). You've seen it happen. In a public setting or a group, someone gets on a roll and doesn't know when to stop. She's wound herself up to such a fever pitch she doesn't sense when the temperature in the room changes. Suddenly those around her begin to shut down because they don't want to touch the conversation with a ten-foot pole. People are offended, and yet the person speaking is totally unaware.

Not only is it offensive when someone cannot bridle her tongue or be sensitive to others in conversation, it is unattractive. The Blueprint says bluntly, "A woman who is beautiful but lacks discretion is like a gold ring in a pig's snout" (Prov. 11:22) unable to discern the value of what they possess. A lack of discretion always looks all wrong, especially when it is coming from a person who looks as if she should know better.

Discretion Keeps You Out of Relationship Trouble

Can we discuss anger? This is a biggie. This is really what got Samson in trouble. After his Philistine in-laws turned on him and gave his wife to another man, he threw a tantrum to rival all tantrums, tying the tails of three hundred foxes together, fastening a torch to each pair, and letting them loose in the crops of the Philistines. In this day and age, that would have had the animal rights people on the warpath, but in that era, ruined crops were enough to almost incite a war.

Samson was cavalier enough to boast that no one should blame him for his behavior because he was a man who had been wronged: "This time I cannot be blamed for everything I am going to do to you Philistines" (Judg. 15:3). Well, to tell the truth, his lack of discretion or good judgment had set him up for this fine mess! He shouldn't have married a non-Israelite to begin with as the law of the day dictated! But he was not about to take responsibility for his bad choice. As many do, Samson chose to blame someone else for his troubles.

Anger out of control opens a man or woman to ruin because good judgment is sure to fly out the window. "People with good sense restrain their anger; they earn esteem by overlooking wrongs" (Prov. 19:11). They choose their battles, placing their words wisely so that they have the right impact. The reason everyone listens when some people speak is because they don't speak that often. You know by the time they say something it is worth hearing.

So stop, listen, think. Check yourself if you feel a rush of words coming on. If you blow it, retrace your steps and make amends. Never be too big to say you're sorry. Check your temper and your responses to situations you don't like. Don't always rush to defend yourself—God will take up your part if you stay in the right position. Don't give in to momentary flushes of passion or desire, but count the cost of your actions and make the right choice. Remember, the amount of discretion you apply to your life will definitely affect the quality of it.

Fits of anger, words spoken in haste, irrational flailing all lead to the same place: certain destruction of a relationship, career, business deal, home, or dream. The bottom line is when we fail to exercise discretion, we place all we hold dear in danger. So be discreet. To live any other way is totally exhausting. Living above the fear of the consequences of your actions overtaking you gives life and invigorates your entire system. Empower yourself by practicing discretion.

The power to stop your life from working will always be up to only one person—that would be you.

CONSTRUCTION TIP
Discretion should be applied liberally to every conversation and action in life. Consider it insulation that protects all that is dear to you. You cannot live without it if you truly want your life to work.

Preventative Maintenance: Diligence

D iligence is all about shrewdly managing all the different areas of your life. You have to manage your home, your finances, your relationships, your physical well-being, your career, you name it. This calls for careful planning and, to some degree, micromanaging. Though delegating is a wonderful thing, you must still spot-check to make sure the details have been handled. This is not something you want to learn the hard way. The hard fact is that no one will be more responsible for your life than you.

If you have great victories, everyone will be there to celebrate them with you. If you suffer defeat and loss, most likely you will be left alone to calculate and ruminate over the devastation. The Blueprint makes it clear:

> Be diligent to know the state
>   of your flocks
> And attend to your herds;
> For riches are not forever,
> Nor does a crown endure to all generations. (Proverbs 27:23–24
>   NKJV)

Never take for granted what you know today. Life changes. You have to be on top of your life! Check and double-check. Be diligent.

We'll look at just three of the areas over which you must keep watch.

Be Diligent with Your Money

In an electronic world, mistakes can occur and much-needed, hard-earned money can slip between the cracks. Enlist financial counsel but also do the work yourself. You will be amazed at the things you find if you check and double-check your credit card and bank statements. Catching a mistake and placing a call is often all it takes to rectify a situation and save you a lot of money.

Small wonder identity theft runs amuck. These people plan on your not paying attention (being diligent) and noticing discrepancies in your credit line.

Don't ignore the warning signs: Bounced checks. Phone calls from creditors. A sudden drop in your credit rating. Regularly take stock, seek financial counsel, make a plan, and do the work to recover before you are in over your head and running for cover from every phone call!

Be Diligent with Your Marriage

Know the state of your "flocks" at home. As small cracks can ruin a foundation and topple a house, small cracks can ruin a relationship and topple a marriage. Recently I was at a conference where I recommended my book *The Power of Being a Woman* to the married women. One woman said to me, "I don't need that book. I've been married for thirty years, and I think I've got it down now."

That was the most naïve comment I had heard in a long time. You should never brag about tomorrow because you don't know what the day will bring, especially if you are not being diligent on your watch (Prov. 27:1).

Every week I hear the same story while traveling to speak to groups of women: husbands walking out of longtime marriages that wives thought were secure. The women stand before me like deer caught in headlights as they voice their dismay at the "sudden" deterioration of their marriages. As I ask questions, realizations begin to surface: "Well, he did say he wasn't happy." "Well, he did say he didn't like this or that." I ask how many times their husbands complained before giving up and falling silent. The Blueprint warns: "Catch us the foxes, the little foxes that spoil the vines, for our vines have tender grapes" (Song of Sol. 2:15 NKJV).

You can never take your relationships for granted. Love must be nurtured and maintained just like the rest of your life. "Too much, too little, too late" is usually the story in too many relationships where couples chose to coast, assuming no news was good news. No news usually means your mate has just found a way to compensate for whatever need you are not meeting. Should he reach a point that the other becomes more satisfying, guess what—you will be replaced! (I am not justifying men or women seeking fulfillment outside their marriages—just warning you about how relationships that aren't diligently maintained can crumble. If you ever give up working at maintaining your marriage, look out.)

I highly recommend diligent management when it comes to your marriage. Watch for changes in your partner's pattern, unreturned calls, late nights at the office, lack of attention, abruptness, impatience, sudden obsession with body image. If their habits suddenly alter drastically, it's time to investigate. Regularly take note of problem areas, and develop a plan and mutual agreement about how to rectify these issues. Hold one another accountable, be honest in your communication, and be determined to help one another do the work it takes to make your relationship continually flourish.

Routine creates safe boundaries for your relationship, but it can also be the death of your relationship. When two hearts shift into automatic, no one notices until too late that love is no longer working. (Read *How to Make Love Work* for more details.)

Be Diligent with Your Children

The notion of letting your children find their way and make their own decisions is foolhardy at best, ludicrous at worst. Kids do not have enough information or wisdom to do this. In God's order, parents are assigned to "train up a child in the way he should go, and when he is old he will not depart from it" (Prov. 22:6 NKJV).

As you train you must enforce. In an age where parents are striving to be friends with their children, I submit to you they are doing a poor job. Their friends know more about what is going on with the kids than their parents do! Children desperately need their parents to set boundaries that keep them safe. You can be friends later, when they become responsible adults—*then* you can finally sit back and see the fruit of your labor.

In diligently raising your children, however, "do not provoke them to wrath" and alienate them (Eph. 6:4 NKJV). Keep communication alive by listening without interrupting and then planting seeds of wisdom or raising questions that cause them to consider your counsel. Again, know the state of your "flocks"—what is going on with your children.

Diligence = Pay Attention

Staying keenly aware of what is going on in every area of your life is key to keeping things running smoothly and avoiding hair-raising

Staying keenly aware of what is going on in every area of your life is key to keeping things running smoothly.

emergencies. Sometimes events short-circuit your plans and redirect you to seek other ways to stay on track and move forward. But we tend to coast on far too many issues.

It is amazing, because the average person likes to feel he or she has control over his or her life, but he or she actually tries to control very little. Perhaps we are all being pulled in too many directions. When you are overwhelmed it is hard to focus on any one thing, but "a prudent person foresees the danger ahead and takes precautions. The simpleton goes blindly on and suffers the consequences" (Prov. 27:12).

Ignorance is not bliss; it is devastating when all that you ignored finally comes to light and you must suffer the consequences.

Pay attention. Clearly see what you are dealing with. Never take surface results for granted: "Only simpletons believe everything they are told! The prudent carefully consider their steps" (Prov. 14:15). It's called walking in wisdom.

Though this may sound like a lot of work, it actually cuts your work to a great degree because it prevents bigger trouble. Diligence will keep a lot of unnecessary drama at bay if utilized in every area of your life. Decide to do the work and reap the benefits.

CONSTRUCTION TIP
Mastering diligence will promote peace, which fortifies your life and keeps it in mint condition.

Preventative Maintenance:
Insight

Sometimes in life you have to go deeper than head knowledge. You have to discern things not from your head but from your spirit. This is a knowing that no one can explain because it comes from beyond ourselves. It is almost a sixth sense. You can't work this one up on your own—this is a God-given thing.

Perception, intuition—whatever you want to call it, you need to have it. It helps you read between the lines of a person's conversation or actions to discern good from evil and the true intent of the person's heart. This discernment is for those who are not happy to just live life as usual. Insight is not a function that everyone uses. This particular practice will set you apart from the pack.

Men of Insight

Let's look at three men in the Manufacturer's Blueprint who had great insight. All were powerful in their own right: Joseph, who interpreted dreams to get out of prison; Solomon, who was known as the wisest man in the world as well as the ruler of Israel back in his day;

and Daniel, who started off as a slave in the palace of the Babylonian king, Nebuchadnezzar, and ended up one of his most trusted advisors and top officials—even though he was a foreigner.

Daniel in particular did something few if any others have ever done: he lasted through five administrations in a key position of power! Do you know the amount of respect you would need to earn for something like that to happen?

Daniel was (literally) able to read the handwriting on the wall when no one else could (Dan. 5). The king, his chief magicians, fortune-tellers, and sorcerers could not. Only Daniel, who had the Spirit of God within him, was able to decipher what God was trying to tell the king. To the enchanters' dismay he didn't even flinch at the prospect of unraveling the mystery.

Joseph had the spiritual insight to interpret the dreams of Pharaoh (Gen. 41). The common denominator is that both Daniel and Joseph set themselves apart to walk in accordance with God's laws. They were both intensely concerned about their relationship with God and pleasing Him.

We know Daniel was a man of prayer. As a matter of fact, all of his colleagues knew it. It was his trademark. They knew he was also a man who would not compromise his faith, no matter what the cost. The same is true of Joseph, who spent unnecessary years in jail because he would not give in to his flesh or the seductive influence of a woman. Because of their focus and commitment to God, these men were highly sensitive in the Spirit.

King Solomon also had great insight—so great in fact that he was renowned the world over. Visitors traveled great distances to see this wonder: "Kings from every nation sent their ambassadors to listen to the wisdom of Solomon" (1 Kings 4:23).

Solomon was also very rich. Insight can be profitable in the business arena. To be able to read the hearts and needs of the people who work with you puts you in a position to win tremendous favor from them. Loyalty heightens productivity, which results in great profit.

Let's look at specific ways insight can help your life work. Solomon in particular shows a variety of benefits.

Ways Insight Helps You Maintain a Life That Works

Insight Helps You Judge Fairly

Insight helps you gauge situations accurately and fairly. I love the story of Solomon's judging between the two women who each claimed the same child as her own. One accused the other of stealing her baby because her own child had been smothered when the mother rolled over it while sleeping. As they haggled back and forth, Solomon declared that they should cut the child in half and each take one-half of the child.

Of course it was never his intention that anyone do so. He knew that the real mother would rather sacrifice her child than see harm done to it and he was right. The one who lied thought dividing the child was a good idea! Guess who went home with the baby?

Whoda thunk to do such a thing? Only a man with great insight.

Insight Inspires Creative Solutions

Insight gives you the ability to creatively find solutions that empower others around you to do the right thing—for example, the idea Solomon offered the two moms fighting over one baby. The more you empower others, as Solomon empowered the real mother to identify herself, the more they love you. These are the ones who become loyal followers, not only willing but happy to follow your leadership and be a part of whatever you are doing.

Insight Gives You a Good Reputation

When the queen of Sheba went to visit Solomon, she assessed not only the words he spoke, she took note of his surroundings as well:

> When she met with Solomon, they talked about everything she had on her mind. Solomon answered all her questions; nothing was too hard for the king to explain to her. When the queen of Sheba realized how wise Solomon was, and when she saw the palace he had built, she was breathless. She was also amazed at the food on his tables, the organization of his officials and their splendid clothing, the cup-bearers and their robes, and the burnt offerings Solomon made at the Temple of the LORD. (1 Kings 10:2–5)

When she saw that everything was in order, running like a finely oiled machine, she was duly impressed.

Somewhere along the way, though, Solomon took a wrong turn. He got just a tad distracted by women—seven hundred wives and three hundred concubines, to be exact—and "they led his heart away from the LORD" (1 Kings 11:3). Did he still have insight? Probably for everyone but himself! After all, he did exactly what God had ordered His people not to: intermarry with foreigners. Insight or no insight, distance from God does not a happy camper make.

Having Insight versus Using Insight

The common thread with all these men who had insight—Joseph, Solomon, and Daniel—is that people thought well of them. Insight gives way to a sterling reputation among your peers and beyond. Perhaps it is because everyone appreciates wisdom graciously extended.

Without it, though you may have a wealth of knowledge, you will offend more than you win.

Many leaders who wield impressive ability as orators and businesspeople miss this one. They, like Solomon, generally start off with the best of intentions. What a wonderful beginning Solomon had! When God offered to give Solomon anything he wanted, he replied, "Give me an understanding mind so that I can govern your people well and know the difference between right and wrong" (1 Kings 3:9). How admirable.

> Insight gives way to a sterling reputation among your peers and beyond.

God obviously thought so, too, since He responded:

> Since you have asked for this and not for long life or wealth for yourself, nor have asked for the death of your enemies but for discernment in administering justice, I will do what you have asked. I will give you a wise and discerning heart, so that there will never have been anyone like you, nor will there ever be. Moreover, I will give you what you have not asked for—both riches and honor—so that in your lifetime you will have no equal among kings. And if you walk in my ways and obey my statutes and commands as David your father did, I will give you a long life. (1 Kings 3:11–14 NIV)

Wow! And yet we've all witnessed the cycle. People start off great but get sidetracked along the way and ultimately fail. Perhaps they begin to believe their own press and turn into completely different people. When you hear the stories of some of our celebrities' employees, it all but sets your hair on fire. There is nothing more disappointing than hearing a negative inside scoop on someone you greatly admire.

People with insight take the time to be led by the Spirit of God and are open to listen to the still, small voice within.

Get Insight

In order to gain insight, win friends, and influence people, you must take the time to cultivate your spiritual hearing. Train yourself to silence the voices without long enough to hear the voice within. Then trust that voice and follow its leading. Repeat what you hear. Allow yourself to become a vessel of the Holy Spirit of God. Open yourself. Let Him fill you and then pour out freely what He has given to others. This is the only source of insight.

The secret to increasing in this area is love. The more you truly care about people, the greater your ability to feel what they feel and hear between the lines of the things they tell you. This is when you will really be able to get to the heart of the matter and nurture life in them. As you give life, you will gain life and that will keep life working for you over the long run.

CONSTRUCTION TIP

Insightful people know that gifts should be used not just for one's own benefit but for others' as well. When you do this, you will ultimately benefit far more than you expected.

Preventative Maintenance: Diet

Make no mistake about it: you are what you eat, physically and spiritually. What you take into your system becomes a part of you and affects everything you do. I touched on this earlier in the book but want to go into more detail here, because many of us struggle with this. For those of us who have been like yo-yos with our weight over the years, we can readily admit our weight had a lot to do with our emotions—our need for comfort, our stress factor, our frame of mind. Perhaps even what we subconsciously thought of ourselves or feared drove us to use food for relief.

Whatever the root cause, the goal is not to be bound to anything in life. Nothing should control your thoughts and emotions other than the Spirit of God, to whom you submit by choice.

My Favorite Things—and Everything Else

Recently I found myself in the position to learn this firsthand. Due to major stresses in my life I was eating everything in sight—my usual favorites along with things I did not normally eat. I placated myself by saying it was the lesser of evils based on what I was going through. But as time passed, I just did not feel good.

Physical Consequences

By two in the afternoon my blood sugar level had dipped drastically. By seven in the evening I was completely depleted, unable to function or stay awake. I also found getting up in the morning difficult. I was the heaviest I had ever been and my limbs were swollen by the end of the day. I was literally dragging myself through life. Easily distracted, I found it hard to focus. All I wanted to do was sleep. I struggled to write. It took everything in me to construct a sentence and afterwards I couldn't tell you what I wrote.

I was heading to the doctor when I decided first to take control of my diet. I began with a cleanse—nothing too drastic, just an herbal tea to purge the system. Then I stripped my diet down to raw vegetables and fruit with small portions of protein. Within three days I could feel the difference. My energy level shot up, the swelling went down. My mind cleared and I was able to get into my normal flow of writing. People noticed the difference and commented that I seemed to be my normal self again. I felt so much better.

I had to accept the fact that sodium and sugar were not my friends and that if I wanted to feel good, I had to discipline myself to stick to a cleaner diet. (Note: Before you do a cleanse or determine a new diet for yourself, always consult a physician.)

Spiritual Consequences

I admit that during the time I was eating badly I found it hard to pray. My mind wandered or I simply had no desire to pray. There were no words. I could hear them in my head but I couldn't get them out. Thank goodness God knows the language of our hearts! I was physically *and* spiritually depleted, unable to make sound decisions. It seemed as if all the important details of my life were falling through the cracks.

After addressing my diet, I was able once again to freely express myself to God and enjoy time with Him. Our Master Architect and Creator sums this up well by saying, "Why spend your money on food that does not give you strength? Why pay for food that does you no good? Listen, and I will tell you where to get food that is good for the soul!" (Isa. 55:2).

It's about More Than Food

This speaks to more than the food you put in your mouth—it speaks to lifestyle. We need to get a healthy perspective on what is truly lasting and fulfilling. In the end we don't just eat food, we eat the fruit of our ways. An unhealthy diet leads not only to health problems, it changes our physical appearance in ways we are not comfortable with. Some people eat to hide because they are afraid of who they become and what they attract when they are smaller; others eat to sedate their pain and comfort themselves. Both lead to becoming overweight and self-defacing. The more uncomfortable people become, the more they eat to comfort themselves; it's a vicious cycle that usually leads to isolation after they become filled not only with food but with shame. They don't feel good; they don't look good; they don't feel good about how they look. Do you see the pattern?

Living comes to a halt. Eating affects relationships as the overeaters withdraw and become less outgoing and active. They suffer in business because the lack of self-confidence makes them passive in the workplace.

I am not a vegetarian, but I am definitely beginning to draw a correlation from the fact that when I eat more fresh, natural foods, that is, vegetables and fruit, I feel more alive.

> In the end we don't just eat food, we eat the fruit of our ways.

My body, mind and spirit are more aligned. I look good, I feel good; I *do* good; if you will.

The Blueprint on Health

The Blueprint offers a telling story about diet with one of my favorite guys, Daniel.

Daniel was brought as a slave, selected because of his pedigree, to the palace of Nebuchadnezzar, the Babylonian king, along with three of his friends: Shadrach, Meshach, and Abednego. These four were among other Israelites who were captured as well.

The four young men refused to eat the delicacies and wine offered to them from the king's kitchen. Knowing those foods weren't acceptable to God, they opted for a very simple diet of vegetables and water. After ten days the difference between the four and the other young men was notable. Daniel and his friends were stronger, healthier, and sharper mentally than their counterparts (Dan. 1).

The point is not that you stick to a diet of water and vegetables. The point is that you take care of your body in a God-honoring way. This will bring blessings into your life. You may not serve in the palace of a king, but you do serve the King of kings and should enjoy the benefits of good health!

The four young men blossomed more than just physically. It appears their dedication to God's ordinances brought about His favor. I'm not talking about the Hollywood kind of favor you earn when you've starved yourself down to a size two. I'm speaking of the favor that comes when you are *aligned within* properly. And God "gave these four young men an unusual aptitude for learning the literature and science of the time. And God gave Daniel special ability in understanding the meanings of visions and dreams" (Dan. 1:17).

How about You?

Perhaps you've experienced some of the physical symptoms I did. Perhaps it's time to reevaluate your health habits. This is not about size. In some cases stick-figure thin is not necessarily healthy. This is about what your body needs so it can function as it should. So take the time to assess how you really feel and adjust your habits and diet accordingly—always in consultation with a physician.

When you take control of your diet, you tell your body and your spirit that food will not have dominion over you. You are the master of your vessel, and what a vessel it is! It is the temple of the Holy Spirit, the place where the Spirit of the Lord abides. He purchased you for his dwelling place, paying an incredibly high price (1 Cor. 6:19–20). Therefore keep it clean and running well. It's the only body you get in this life and how it runs will affect everything else—and that, my friend, should be motivation enough to get your act together because when all has been said and done, you'll need your body in order for your life to work.

CONSTRUCTION TIP
Your body does not belong to you. It belongs to the Master Architect, and every landlord likes to find his property in the same condition in which he "rented" it.

Preventative Maintenance: Rest

N othing on the face of the earth can operate perpetually. It will run out of batteries, blow a fuse, finish its season, or just fail to perform any longer. The mind, body, and spirit must have rest. Let's face it—even God rested. What does that tell you? If the Creator of all things found it necessary to call a time-out, how much do we as mere mortals need time for renewal, revival, and restoration? It is the natural order of the universe that we incorporate rest into our schedules. It is the law of tension and release, of life and death, of seedtime and harvest.

The Master Creator ordered the Israelites to plant for six years and then give the earth a rest in the seventh year. Anticipating their concern for provision in the year they did not plant, He said:

> You may ask, "What will we eat in the seventh year if we do not plant or harvest our crops?" I will send you such a blessing in the sixth year that the land will yield enough for three years. While you plant during the eighth year, you will eat from the old crop and will continue to eat from it until the harvest of the ninth year comes in. (Leviticus 25:20–22 NIV)

But they didn't believe Him, so they planted right up to the time they were taken away to Babylon into captivity. Because of this, the

Lord decreed that they would remain in slavery until the land had caught up on all the rest it should have had—seventy years' worth, to be exact (2 Chron. 36:21)! The moral of the story? Rest by choice or you will rest by force. Nature and your system have a way of telling you when enough is enough.

Why was God so concerned about the earth's getting its rest? Because He knew that constant planting would deplete the soil of its nutrients, which would result in substandard (less tasty and nutritious) crops. The earth needed to replenish itself in order to produce succulent vegetation.

The earth is a lot like us. When we are spiritually, mentally, and physically depleted, we, too, fail to produce our best.

Burnout Destroys, Rest Renews

Have you ever noticed that after you've pushed yourself beyond your natural limits, it seems as if your body will never catch up on the rest it needs? This is called burnout. Burnout shuts down your ability to function well in every area of life. Relationships suffer because weariness does not promote patience. Business suffers because a tired mind is an unfocused mind. Shall I go on? You get the general picture. When you are tired, you make bad decisions. Some of them could affect your life forever, while others bear short-term consequences that may not be pleasant either.

The tyranny of the urgent would deceive you into thinking you can't afford to rest because of all you have to do. I have two answers for that. First, you can't afford *not* to rest. Second, if you have that much going on, there is something on your plate that shouldn't be.

Stop, take a deep breath, and ponder what is before you. For every false obligation you've embraced, something in your life is suffering. Make a list of everything you have to do. Number the list in order of importance. If you had to cut the list in half, which things would remain as essentials? What is the order of importance of those things remaining if you apply yourself at a reasonable pace?

The fallacy is that no one is dispensable, yet people die every day and life goes on without them. Harsh, but true. We take a moment to mourn those lost but we've still got lives to lead.

Don't Get Too Stressed to Be Blessed

There has to be more to life than just going through the motions, constantly performing—and there is. For as much as the Master Architect has built us to be fruitful, He also wants us to take the time to enjoy the fruit of our labor and the rest of His creation. It is when we are at rest that He is able to plant new seeds in our spirits: to water us with His Spirit, nurture us with His Word, and refresh us by revealing His goodness and creativity. This should spur us on to greater heights of creativity of our own, which will bring fulfillment as we become conduits of blessings for others and make contributions to the world around us.

But when we are too stressed to be blessed, we have a problem. If we can't let go of life every now and then, God can't add anything to it—our hands are closed. Rest assured (no pun intended), He will not pry your hands open and force you to be blessed! He will look elsewhere for open hands, hearts, and spirits instead.

Admittedly, resting goes against society's demands, which are driven by what one can *do* instead of what one can *be*. Yet we must remember that God wants us to "do" the Word: "Do not merely listen to the word, and so deceive yourselves.

> When we are too stressed to be blessed, we have a problem.

Do what it says" (James 1:22 NIV). After that He calls us to *be*: "Be holy, for I am holy" (Lev. 11:44 NASB). "*Be* still, and know that I am God" (Ps. 46:10 NKJV). "If any man *be* in Christ, he is a new creature" (2 Cor. 5:17 KJV).

See? Be, be, be...be a being! That is so much simpler that *doing* everything. Perhaps this is why Jesus extends such a wonderful invitation to everyone, saying, "Come to me, all you who are weary and burdened, and I will give you rest. Take my yoke upon you and learn from me, for I am gentle and humble in heart, and you will find rest for your souls. For my yoke is easy and my burden is light" (Matt. 11:28–30 NIV).

Our Creator is not a harsh taskmaster. It is His wish that our lives be a testimony of His goodness and faithfulness. God's image is affected when we don't operate at our best—when our lives aren't working. What you do well in life also affects the kingdom of heaven. After all, who will want to go there if all of its citizens look worse for wear? That is simply not good PR for a fabulous destination.

One year I visited Monte Carlo. What an amazing and beautiful place. It was immaculate. The citizens all looked so happy. I was told that citizens of Monte Carlo did not pay taxes. After taking in all of the scenery and wonderful conditions, I decided that the prince of Monte Carlo was a pretty cool guy. For a moment I wanted to be a citizen.

We should always be cognizant of whom we ultimately represent. We are the proof that God is good. And we can reflect that only when we are well rested and fully charged for life.

Rest Defined

Rest is different things to different people. Simply put, rest is taking a break from effort and thought, focus and energy. Perhaps for you that is sitting somewhere enjoying music; for someone else it's a long, leisurely walk through a park or along a seashore. Rest is quieting your mind, your spirit, and your body, ceasing and desisting from further activity that requires output.

Now let's put another spin on rest. How about this? Rest is having absolute confidence in God to take care of the things that are causing you concern. Anxiety puts undue stress on your body and mind. Release your cares to Him because He cares for you (1 Pet. 5:7). Rest from all that concerns you and leave it with Him. Then your life will work.

CONSTRUCTION TIP
This is one maintenance detail you cannot get around. If you don't take the time to rest, physically, mentally, and even spiritually, life will stop you and at that point, everything will stop working.

Preventative Maintenance: Balance

Night and day, darkness and light, tension and release: all are opposites yet they bring much-needed balance to the world. Consider what life would be like if it were night all the time, or day. They are both necessary to bring balance to the universe. It is part of the order of God. When all the elements are in harmony, they bring perfect balance to the earth and all of its inhabitants.

On the personal side, balance is the act of juggling all the balls at the same time: personal and professional, giving and saving, work and play, feeling and thinking, spiritual and natural. Where should the real emphasis be? Does one outweigh the other?

How do we make wise choices so we don't go to one extreme or another? How can we keep our lives not just functioning but functioning optimally? The thing that will help you maintain consistency in your life is balance.

All of You Is Important

It is important not to ignore any part of you.

Your Spirit

There is the delicate balance between spiritual and natural. Many people are so "spiritual," or heavenly minded, that they are no earthly good—they pray a lot and quote Scriptures about righteousness but don't help the needy in front of them. While others are so fleshly minded they do no spiritual good—they help the poor but never take the time to nurture their spirits or their relationships with God. Some kind of balance between the two is what we should strive for.

Your Body

Taking care of your body is another issue. You should maintain its health without obsessing about it. Your health matters, but developing your physical attributes as a primary goal is unbalanced. Beauty is fleeting. Nature takes its natural course in aging and though many try to defy it today, it eventually catches up with all of us.

Balance calls us to take care of the outer but also nurture the inner beauty of our spirits. It is amazing but true: some of the most physically beautiful people in the world have the least-attractive personalities. Their attitudes actually mar their perfect finish. The pursuits of beauty and character must balance for life to work.

Your Possessions

The outer trappings always seem to get us in trouble. If we're not obsessed with body image and fabulous fashion, we get carried away with the things we acquire. Material possessions are wonderful but are also a trivial pursuit if they are your primary focus. Possessions come and go. The key is to own them but not let them own you.

Any possession for which you have to go into unnecessary debt is something not worth having. Don't let greed outweigh your good sense. Be realistic about what are needs and what are wants; this is the first step to making wiser choices about how you spend your money—and what you base your life on.

Your Achievements

Keeping achievements in perspective is also important. Famous people eventually fall from prominence. Many have difficulty adjusting to anonymity. You can be on top of the world today and plummet into oblivion tomorrow. You never know when you are going to be the flavor of the month, or a shooting star that burns out after momentary brilliance. The most famous of people have been at the forefront of the news one day and a year later they are on the "Whatever happened to…" list. Understand that life is seasonal; this is crucial to maintaining a steady, even keel.

Everything Has a Season

This is the Blueprint's description of balance:

> [There is] a time to be born and a time to die,
> a time to plant and a time to uproot,
> a time to kill and a time to heal,
> a time to tear down and a time to build,
> a time to weep and a time to laugh,
> a time to mourn and a time to dance,
> a time to scatter stones and a time to gather them,
> a time to embrace and a time to refrain,
> a time to search and a time to give up,
> a time to keep and a time to throw away,
> a time to tear and a time to mend,
> a time to be silent and a time to speak,
> a time to love and a time to hate,
> a time for war and a time for peace. (Ecclesiastes 3:2–8 NIV)

We often wonder, can we really have it all? The answer is sure we can, just not all at the same time. We can juggle only so many demands at once. The question is whether our priorities are straight.

When traveling abroad I'm always amazed at how relational people seem to be, more so than in America. They put work on hold for the sake of relationship. They are much more interested in the quality of life than the quantity of possessions that would require working longer hours. They have six weeks of vacation a year!

They believe in living balanced lives. They work hard, yes, but also take time to smell the roses, see the world, invest time in their relationships. They even take longer to eat meals, allowing for meaningful conversations. They take siestas in the middle of the day! Such people truly enjoy life.

Is money important? Yes, we all want to eat. But how much money do we really need? Though the writer of Ecclesiastes noted that lazy people believe "money is the answer for everything" (Eccl. 10:19 NIV), it is also true that money can bring its own set of problems.

Is your career important? Yes, it is wonderful to exercise your gifts. But is your career the only thing that defines or validates you? Since you can't serve two masters equally—you will love one and despise the other—be careful that your job does not rob you of relationship with the One who is the Giver of validation—God (Matt. 6:24).

Is your marriage or your significant other important? Of course! Love should be a priority; relationships are crucial to our existence. But is that person your only source of esteem? Would you be any less of who you are if that person were not there?

Keeping things in the right order leads to balance.

Keeping things in the right order leads to balance. Family is more important than career. Career is more important than hobby. Spiritual health is more important than physical health. But they are all important! Don't let others lead you off course or trick you into overcommitting yourself. It's been said if the devil can't make you bad, he will make you busy.

Balance can be a tricky thing. Our companions, health, attitudes, stresses, pleasures, perspectives, and more change as life unfolds. But remember that God will give you grace for all you encounter. Remember He said His yoke is easy. Don't take on other people's assignments. There is a difference between embracing responsibility and drowning in false obligation. If you need to, stop—let all the balls fall. Revisit your priorities and prayerfully ask God to help you rearrange them in the proper order. Pick them back up, adjust your stance, and begin the juggle once again.

Peace instead of conflict: that is the goal. This will keep your life working no matter what happens.

CONSTRUCTION TIP
Without balance, you are unstable. An unstable person is dangerous to themselves and others. A life that works requires prioritizing and smart balance.

Long-Term Maintenance:
Self-Control

We live in a rebellious society that abhors rules and boundaries. However, when you step back and objectively look at the way things work, you will discover that rules are good. They keep you safe, focused, and on track. They make it easier to maintain a vital practice: exercising self-control. This one thing can make or break your life.

Self-control refers to the self-assigned rules that help you accomplish your goals. The failure to exercise discipline can cost you greatly. No, I take that back; it can cost you everything: your health, your relationships, your career, your financial standing. Self-control insulates your life. It keeps in everything that should be kept in—strong faith, good friends, consistently smart decision making—and keeps out everything that should be kept out—doubt, draining relationships, and indecisiveness. You will have to use discipline as part of your daily maintenance—for the rest of your life.

When it comes to discipline, you can swing from one extreme to another. You can either start everything and finish nothing or totally overdo things to your own demise. Discipline involves not only starting that diet, that financial plan, that relationship, that new job search, it is the follow-through to the finish. Finishing what you start is key to life working. Being faithful in the little things opens the door to your becoming ruler over much. Brilliance is short-lived if it cannot be utilized in completing your mission.

Lack of discipline leads to many regrets and unfinished works, robbing you of the satisfaction you could have if you chose to apply due diligence. Usually at the root of a lack of self-discipline is a fear of success or low self-esteem. If you find yourself a great starter but a poor finisher, you need to examine yourself to see if either of these culprits is at work. You need to circumvent self-destructive behavior. Be honest: are you sabotaging your own life by refusing to finish what you begin? Or are you at the other extreme, refusing to rein in your impulses, again greatly damaging your life?

Who Is in Charge?

The temptation to overindulge or underperform will never go away. The Master Architect designed you to have basic desires along with the ability to be able to master those desires—to refuse to allow anything to reign over you but Him:

> Think of it this way: Sin speaks a dead language that means nothing to you; God speaks your mother tongue, and you hang on every word. You are dead to sin and alive to God. That's what Jesus did.
>
> That means you must not give sin a vote in the way you conduct your lives. Don't give it the time of day. Don't even run little errands that are connected with that old way of life. Throw yourselves wholeheartedly and full-time—remember you've been raised from the dead!—into God's way of doing things. *Sin can't tell you how to live.* (Romans 6:12–14 *The Message*, italics mine)

Therefore you have to make up your mind every day, if not every hour, to use wisdom instead of giving in to excess. Remember, it is fine to have desires—they just should not have you.

It is important to understand the economy of balance that tells us everything is allowed but not expedient or edifying. Paul wrote, "All things are lawful for me, but not all things are profitable. All things are lawful for me, but I will not be mastered by anything" (1 Cor. 6:12 NASB). You can eat as much as you want, but what will overeating do to your body and overall health? You can buy anything you want, but what will happen to your finances and your future? So many things are fun, exciting, or actually good for you—but taken in extreme they can all become destructive.

Where You Need Self-Control

Basically, self-control must be applied to every area of your lifestyle, from your mind to your tongue, your conversation, your eating, your spending—you name it. As Mama used to say, "What's good *to* you isn't necessarily good *for* you." Let's take a look at some specific areas where discipline can benefit you.

The Mind

There is a reason Paul wrote in the Blueprint, "We are destroying speculations and every lofty thing raised up against the knowledge of God, and we are taking every thought captive to the obedience of Christ" (2 Cor. 10:5 NASB). Let's dissect that idea. *The Message* says we should be "smashing warped philosophies, tearing down barriers erected against the truth of God, fitting every loose thought and emotion and impulse into the structure of life shaped by Christ."

This sums it up perfectly. Whether we are resisting the call of God to our lives or just interacting with others on a daily basis, we are to be on the lookout for "warped philosophies," wrong thinking, and negative attitudes that can erect major barriers to our getting the results we want in our work, our relationships, and our goals. Loose thoughts based on assumptions and our impulsive reactions can cause a lot of misunderstandings.

Watch any movie or soap opera to see how this drama can play out. She thought he was cheating on her, so she ran to find comfort in the arms of another man. While crying about *him* in the other man's embrace, the man she is crying over sees her in the arms of another man and *assumes* that she is cheating on *him*, thus the cycle of heartbreak continues in a hot mess that was completely unnecessary! We find ourselves sitting in front of the television yelling for someone to tell somebody what really happened, but it doesn't happen until many years after they've broken up and married other people. Then they discover they still love one another—it was all a misunderstanding! Whew! All that drama for nothing. Who needs it?

Our minds can run rampant with inaccurate information, causing us to make devastating choices if we don't reel them in. Stop imagining and get to the heart of the matter by utilizing another wonderful tool the Master Architect has given you called *communication*. (Learn more about this in the manual *How to Make Love Work*.)

The Tongue

Speaking of communication, watch those words! Our tongues can get us in a heap of trouble if we don't exercise discipline. Not everything we hear, see, or feel does needs to be vocalized. Even if it is the truth, sometimes it is better left unsaid. You should "keep your tongue from evil and your lips from speaking deceit" (Ps. 34:13 NASB). Sometimes the things we say are not necessarily evil; they may be true, but they bear evil fruit—i.e., hurt feelings, strife, broken relationships, a fresh round of gossip. We are to have no slander on our tongues and no nasty things to say about our friends (Ps. 15:3).

This means no gossiping, no backbiting, no repeating what you've heard. "He who repeats a matter separates friends" (Prov. 17:9 NKJV). How many times has someone said to you, "Don't repeat this, but..."? Practice self-discipline about what you allow yourself to hear if you know you won't be able to harbor matters in your heart. It is an act of discipline to keep the secrets and the trust of others. Truly the power of life and death is in the tongue (Prov. 18:21)!

Remember that as offspring of the Master Architect, we have inherited the same creative power He has. Our words are creative energy igniting a spark or train of events that can corrupt a whole person and set the whole course of a life on fire. The flip side of that is the tongue can be used to bring healing, reconciliation, and restoration—it can be a source of life. This is why we are encouraged to keep a tight rein on our tongues.

The Blueprint says, "Whoever would love life and see good days must keep his tongue from evil and his lips from deceitful speech" (1 Pet. 3:10 NIV). Guarding your words and the impulse to say whatever is on your mind is an act of discipline that few, if any, completely master. Taming the tongue takes a lifetime. Purpose to achieve this goal. It will change your life—and help it keep working!

The Body

We are called to crucify the flesh daily. Though we are encouraged to present our bodies as a living sacrifice, pleasing and acceptable to God as a reasonable act of worship or thanks for all that He has done for us (Rom. 12:1), it is easier said than done. Even the mighty apostle Paul, who wrote most of the New Testament, complained,

> I do not understand what I do. For what I want to do I do not do, but what I hate I do. And if I do what I do not want to do, I agree that the law is good. As it is, it is no longer I myself who do it, but it is sin living in me. I know that nothing good lives

in me, that is, in my sinful nature. For I have the desire to do what is good, but I cannot carry it out. For what I do is not the good I want to do; no, the evil I do not want to do—this I keep on doing. (Romans 7:15–19 NIV)

He concluded that he had to die daily to his own desires. This means we not only take responsibility for our nature and desires but that we consciously give God our bodies, lay down the urges that go against His instructions for our lives, yielding in complete obedience to Him.

The only problem with a living sacrifice is that it keeps crawling off the altar, wandering after what it wants. Each and every day we have to remind ourselves whom we are subject to. Nothing just happens: every act starts with a thought (the mind) that slides down to our hearts, which influence us to make our bodies follow the desire we've become focused on. Those who are focused on the flesh obey the flesh, but those who focus on the Spirit obey the Spirit of God within them (Rom. 8:5). It is only when we crucify the flesh with its passions and lusts (Gal. 5:24) and follow after the Spirit that true life floods our beings (Rom. 8:13); therefore we should "make no provision" for the demands of the flesh (Rom. 13:14 NASB).

We must exercise the power we've been given to silence the selfish cries of our flesh and yield to an even greater power, that of the Spirit of the Master Creator and Architect. The apostle Paul put it this way:

> The only problem with a living sacrifice is that it keeps crawling off the altar, wandering after what it wants.

You've all been to the stadium and seen the athletes race. Everyone runs; one wins. Run to win. All good athletes train hard. They do it for a gold medal that tarnishes and fades. You're after one that's gold eternally.

I don't know about you, but I'm running hard for the finish line. I'm giving it everything I've got. No sloppy living for me! I'm staying alert and in top condition. (1 Corinthians 9:24–27 *The Message*)

This is the height of taking responsibility for your actions—practicing self-control. The Master Creator has given you the power to do this. You should never say, "This is just the way I am." You have the power to redirect your focus, cast off your inclinations, put on Christ, and exercise dominion over every part of your being. (And if you simply can't practice self-control on your own, seek out professionals who can help you do so.)

"Putting on Christ" simply means choosing to imitate Him rather than following the leading of the world. Though you may be marching contrary to others, consider the fact that you hear a different drummer who is beating out a better song that you can feel coursing through your veins; it's called the song of life.

CONSTRUCTION TIP
Remain diligent. Should you become too comfortable or think too highly of yourself, you will lose the urgent desire to practice self-control. And then you'll fail to maintain a life that works.

Long-Term Maintenance: Perseverance

Many pray for patience but few utilize it. We live in an instant-gratification society, yet most things of lasting value are not created overnight. A popular advertisement back in the seventies showed the owner of a vineyard proclaiming he would "sell no wine before its time." His reputation was on the line. The flavor of his wine would be a reflection of his mastery.

And so it is with our lives: the Master Architect is more interested in the quality than in the quantity of accomplishments or the speed with which they're achieved. The race is given not to the swift but to those who endure to the end. It's one thing to run, but can you finish?

Perseverance is an essential form of maintenance simply because things happen that will try you, press you, and even push you over the edge. If you throw up your hands and cave in every time an adverse condition hits, life will be over before it can ever really begin.

There is a popular myth running rampant in the world—and even more so in Christianity—that life is supposed to be easy and perfect, especially if you know the Lord. That is stated *nowhere* in the Master Blueprint. As a matter of fact, before Jesus departed from the earth, He said something quite to the contrary: "In the world you will have tribulation; but be of good cheer, I have overcome the world" (John 16:33 NKJV).

That, my friend, is the nitty-gritty reality of life. We live in a fallen world full of sin that will stretch us and hopefully grow us up into the mature people we were created to be.

We Need Hardship

"What?" you may be asking. We do—we need tough times. Take a look at all the spoiled brats in the world. Their lack of character is proof enough that the "perfect" life does not necessarily produce perfection or maturity. Every trial God allows us to go through—the operative words being *go through* as opposed to *escape*—arrives by divine design, allowed into our lives to perfect three things in us: our faith, our perspective, and our character. Without life rubbing us the wrong way at times, we would never grow into the greatness God has planned for us.

It is the strain that makes us stronger, able to endure and withstand more. With each trial, if we lean harder into God and His Blueprint, we become more and more who we were created to be. As you build your life, construct it with patience. Make sure that you are able to withstand the greatest test—that of time.

> Without life rubbing us the wrong way at times, we would never grow into the greatness God has planned for us.

Perseverance is what you need. It is a special grace that operates in hard times for believers, taking them beyond what they can bear. When we feel as if life is stretching us beyond our limits—and yet we find the strength to stand firm, take a licking, and keep on ticking—we are developing perseverance. This ability to endure against the odds is a testimony to the faithfulness of God and His keeping power that covers us not only in this life but in the world to come as well.

Wear and Tear's Effect on a Strong Spirit

Have you ever met an elderly person whose body was worn out but her mind was still sharp as a whip? She could recall things and events that no one else could, still beat you at a board game, and still have a comeback line for anything you uttered. Not only did she have wisdom beyond her years; she exuded power even though she seemed frail in physical makeup. She had a gleam in her eye that revealed hidden vitality from another source.

I had a grandmother like that. The older she got, she seemed to "go from strength to strength" (Ps. 84:7 NIV). God is our power, and He is the one who makes our way "perfect" (2 Sam. 22:33 NIV). Perhaps God's perfection looks quite different from what you imagined it should. God orchestrates our lives to bring out the best in us, to beautify us with His holiness. All stresses and hits are designed to define and align us in such a way that we reflect His glory and greatness. Sometimes that means a trial is necessary to break us down and make room for the overhaul that must occur. In my grandmother's eyes was a calm assurance based on years of experiencing the faithfulness of God. People were drawn to her and did not know why, but I do. She had a quiet strength and peace that was so beautiful it was like a magnet. People sought her out for comfort and strength.

She had a certainty about who she was and where she was going because the fear of the Lord was her "strong confidence" (Prov. 14:26 NKJV). She knew that though her physical body would not last forever, her spirit would.

So how do you want to spend the rest of your life? What do you want reflected in your eyes when you are elderly, like my grand-mother? We need divine perspective. If we commit to walking and living in a righteous fashion despite any challenges, that brings God pleasure and strengthens us for whatever is ahead. We will live life on a higher level where all that we learn in this world will prepare us for the next. We will finally be perfect—perfected to live in a perfect world. Perseverance is the way.

What's a Race without a Finish?

To make the initial investment and then not hang around to see the finished product should be a crime in itself. Just think how God feels when we try to shortcut the process of development and rob ourselves of becoming all we could be. The couple who bail out of a marriage because the relationship gets too hard never learn how to make love work. The person who walks off a job before payday will never feel the satisfaction of cashing a well-earned check. In short, you need to persevere so that when you have done the will of God you will receive what He has promised (Heb. 10:36).

Honor is never given to those who bail. Kudos are given to those who refuse to turn back in the face of adversity. Patiently pressing forward, these people keep their heads when all around them people are abdicating their posts. People who persevere stay focused on the goal.

The early saints, as described in Hebrews 11, kept their focus on Jesus, our prime example: "Jesus, the author and finisher of our faith, who for the joy that was set before Him endured the cross, despising the shame, and has sat down at the right hand of the throne of God" (Heb. 12:2 NKJV). That's what I'm talking about: sticking and staying, getting your hard-earned reward.

Whether you struggle with getting a professional promotion, achieving weight loss, establishing a fabulous marriage, raising children who do you proud, finishing a difficult project, or overcoming in a wrestling match with your faith, understand that simple perseverance is key to enjoying victory. Our predecessors listed in Hebrews 11 pressed on no matter what they faced: "Through acts of faith, they toppled kingdoms, made justice work, took the promises for themselves. They were protected from lions, fires, and sword thrusts, turned disadvantage to advantage, won battles, routed alien armies." In short, they "[made] their way as best they could on the cruel edges of the world" (Heb. 11:33–34, 38 *The Message*).

Paul himself wrote, "Friends, don't get me wrong: by no means do I count myself an expert in all of this, but I've got my eye on the goal, where God is beckoning us onward—to Jesus. I'm off and running, and I'm not turning back. . . . Now that we're on the right track, let's stay on it" (Phil. 3:13–14, 16 *The Message*).

People in the Bible who earned great acclaim did not allow themselves to be deterred by naysayers or even by their own discouragement. They were able to bypass immediate gratification in exchange for something better. They kept their focus on the real deal, the prize up ahead—the fulfillment that awaited them if they simply endured. James wrote, "Anyone who meets a testing challenge head-on and manages to stick it out is mighty fortunate. For such persons are loyally in love with God, the reward is life and more life" (James 1:12 *The Message*).

How to Endure

So how do we become those who get "life and more life"? How do we get good at taking our knocks but never giving up?

1. Accept It
Accepting the fact that life is hard is the first step to building endurance. If you anticipate that things won't be easy, you won't be thrown

when they aren't. This is why the Master Architect's Blueprint clearly states: "We can rejoice, too, when we run into problems and trials, for we know that they are good for us—they help us learn to endure. And endurance develops strength of character in us, and character strengthens our confident expectation of salvation. And this expectation will not disappoint us" (Romans 5:3–5).

This flies in the face of a lot of modern-day theology, doesn't it? The announcement has gone out that we are not supposed to suffer; that anything or anybody who makes us suffer is bad. Nothing worthwhile comes from suffering. We should feel great all the time. Yet the One who made us says that suffering is *good*.

How can suffering be good? Consider how physical trainers encourage us to "feel the burn." The burn tells us we're building muscle. Stretching hurts, yet it yields positive results in our lives—the muscles of character, grace, and integrity. The fruit of rich marriages, of dreams finally realized, of children you can be proud of, of financial security, of healthy bodies—these are all good things attainable by endurance.

2. Dance in Advance

Next, build endurance by counting it all joy. Yes! Dance in advance, because trial is a good indication that something in your life is worth fighting for. Anticipate the victory and be ready to embrace it. Trust God to give you enough strength to pass the test with flying colors. When you feel weak, ask for His strength. And expect that all will come out all right; walk in the full assurance that God is faithful and nurture a grateful heart ahead of time.

3. Practice, Practice, Practice

Perseverance can be worked into your system only by practice. It is said that time heals all things; it also reveals all things and works all things out in us. You will never see the full picture of your life if you don't persevere through the building process. You will never learn the lessons you need to learn if God delivers you from every trial without using the circumstance to teach and perfect you.

Case in point: it is documented that many lottery winners quickly go bankrupt. Why? Because winning a lot of money doesn't guarantee you know how to manage or grow riches. But take people who have suffered through severe debt, who finally make it to financial freedom and learn their lesson: they will be much more circumspect with their money.

This is why enduring is so valuable. It prepares you for blessing in the future. You will miss this if you refuse to endure—persevere through—the trials and tests of life. If you can consistently accept, prepare for, and dance in spite of problems, you are well on your way to building endurance—and a life that always works.

CONSTRUCTION TIP

If you feel you can't make it through your test, tell yourself you can and then you will. Make sure you have the right support system— lean on the Others and Purpose Cornerstones—to help you endure. It always helps to have a cheering section!

Long-Term Maintenance: Godliness

You've met them: men and women who looked far younger than their years. No lines creased their faces, as if they had never had a worry or a care. You've quietly vowed to yourself to look that good when you get to be their age.

When asked how they did it, perhaps you too got the reply, "Clean living!" You pondered what choices led to such radiant results. They were not always people with a lot of money or material things, yet they possessed peace and joy—probably their greatest beauty secrets. A simple maintenance program of godly living proved worthwhile. Truly "godliness with contentment is great gain" (1 Tim. 6:6 NIV).

So how can you use this form of maintenance to keep your life working?

How to Get Godly

1. Be Grateful

Godliness is reflected in a heart grateful for all its blessings. No matter where you are, or what you think you lack, there is something to be thankful for right now. Gratefulness takes stock of all you *do* have without considering what you *don't*. Right now you have it better than most, even though you may not feel you do. I dare you: actually count your blessings. I guarantee that if you're paying attention, you'll run out of numbers before you run out of blessings to count!

For some guidance, check out Psalm 103. Nurture a grateful heart and don't forget the benefits God has bestowed upon you.

> Consistent gratefulness in spite of your circumstances proves you trustworthy to be blessed and births a true sense of contentment.

As you walk in thankfulness, celebrating what He has done and how He has sustained you through difficult times, you make room for more blessings to follow. Consistent gratefulness in spite of your circumstances proves you trustworthy to be blessed and births a true sense of contentment.

2. Obey Him

Godliness is a reverence for God's goodness that translates itself into right living before Him as your simple way of saying "Thank You" for all He has done for you. Jesus said, "If you love me, you will obey what I command" (John 14:15 NIV). There it is: *show Me how much you love Me.* Godly living is the reflection of God in our everyday lives.

True relationship with and love for the Master Architect and a true understanding of His Blueprint should make you uncomfortable to be ungodly. John the apostle put it this way: "Those who have been born into God's family do not sin, because God's life is in them. So they can't keep on sinning, because they have been born of God" (1 John 3:9). It doesn't get any clearer than that. To live any other way is to be at war with the Christlike nature that abides in you.

3. Seek Him

"As we know Jesus better, his divine power gives us everything we need for living a godly life" (2 Pet. 1:3). By adopting the mind-set of Christ, loving what He loves and hating what He hates—deciding not to embrace what is offensive to Him—godliness becomes an integral part of who we are, as natural as breathing. We are empowered to be godly. As we consume the Word of God, it goes into our system and becomes a part of our blood, the very fiber of our being. We are what we eat; what we consume, consumes us. Godliness is no longer something we have to think about.

I call it God Automatic. This is the evidence that our nature is truly changed. Godliness is evident to all we meet because the godly not only feed their own lives with good things, they give life to others too. Through wise counsel, an upright example, and the rich fruit of all you do, others will recognize something different about you. Though they may not know what that "something" is, they will know that they want it. Godliness spreads beyond you to effect change in the lives of others, leaving a rich legacy that continues to give life long after you are gone.

4. Study the Blueprint

Because you've chosen to embrace God and live according to His ways, study His Blueprint for your life. That knowledge will change your mind, which should change your choices. When I first gave my life to Christ and began to read the Word of God, it was like taking off dark sunglasses on an extremely sunny day. I found myself squinting in the light of the glaring truth of what some of my choices had afforded me. It was jolting to realize how misguided I had been in some of my personal philosophies. What was I thinking?

My former way of life became distasteful to me. It no longer held delight or amusement for me because I knew the end of the matter. This is a good example of how knowledge can aid in becoming godly. If you knew there was poison in your soup, you would not eat it, would you? Armed with new knowledge, I deliberately chose to go right instead of left and found the peace that welcomed me absolutely amazing.

Want to get godly? Go straight to the source. Study the Blueprint and follow its directions for godly living.

5. Get Rid of the Junk

If you are trying to build and maintain a godly life, you must remove everything that is not conducive to peace, joy, and all that preserves your sanity. The wrong people, the wrong choices, the wrong mind-sets—they all have to go. The Manufacturer's Blueprint suggests that if your right hand causes you to sin, cut it off (metaphorically speaking) (Matt. 5:30). Get rid of anything harmful to yourself and others.

Have you left room for God to move in your life, or have you filled every part of your existence with things and people that crowd Him out? Can you clearly hear His voice and follow His instruction? A well-maintained life has closed out the clutter.

Benefits of Godly Living: He Is So into You!

Maintaining a life of godliness places you front and center with God. He takes personal interest in all the intricacies of your life. Not only does He protect and keep you, making sure you have all you need spiritually and naturally, but "the steps of the godly are directed by the LORD. He delights in every detail of their lives" (Ps. 37:23). Every detail! That's huge!

As I mentioned earlier, it is the little foxes that ruin the vine: the little things that creep in unnoticed do the most damage. The erosion in a marriage, a business, or any situation of import has usually done its worst work before anyone notices. By then it is too late not to suffer the repercussions. These are the details God likes to oversee, before the dry rot sets in. Only by drawing close to Him, allowing Him to point out the areas we need to pay attention to, following His direction, and making godly choices do we reap the benefits of a life sustained by godliness.

Godliness should be evident in every fiber of your being. It should resonate in every word you speak, causing every aspect of your life to flourish and every gain to be sustained: "The reward of the godly will last" (Prov. 11:18). Why? Because this is the substance of life! "The godly are like trees that bear life-giving fruit" (Prov. 11:30). "The way of the godly leads to life; their path does not lead to death" (Prov. 12:28).

Life! That is what godliness is all about. It is within our power to choose whether we flourish or we die.

Godliness is not pie in the sky, an overly lofty goal. It is basic to everyday living and something that you must consciously pursue, knowing that "godliness has value for all things, holding promise for both the present life and the life to come" (1 Tim. 4:8 NIV).

The benefits speak for themselves: a quality of life sustainable because your way is guarded by God Himself. He watches over your finances, your relationships, your possessions, health, security, everything! Godliness is the best life insurance on the planet. Though it does not exempt you from trouble, it does guarantee the intervention of God on your behalf no matter what you suffer.

While you are alive you experience the benefits of His care and watchfulness. When you die you enter into His rest. You can't lose either way, and that is when you know that life is truly working.

CONSTRUCTION TIP
You need to incorporate godliness into every aspect of your life. Without it, every area of life is vulnerable to corruption.

Long-Term Maintenance: Love

The whole world is in love with the concept of love. Small wonder. We were created by Love for the purpose of loving. Love should bleed from the interior to the exterior of your life and change the face of every person you encounter. Love should be your trademark:

> Anyone who loves is born of God and knows God. But anyone who does not love does not know God—for God is love.... Dear friends, since God loved us that much, we surely ought to love each other. No one has ever seen God. But if we love each other, God lives in us, and his love has been brought to full expression through us. (1 John 4:7–8, 11–12)

Love should be where you live and invite others to come. It is our way of responding to the love God has extended to us.

> We love each other as a result of his loving us first. If someone says, "I love God," but hates a Christian brother or sister, that person is a liar; for if we don't love people we can see, how can we love God, whom we have not seen? And God himself has commanded that we must love not only him but our Christian brothers and sisters, too. (1 John 4:19–21)

And beyond our brothers and sisters, we are to love *all* of our fellow inhabitants of the planet Earth! Believers and unbelievers. Sinners and saints. This is what Jesus did. In the heat of their religious obsession, the Pharisees had serious problems with that; they preferred to "love" only those they deemed worthy. But Jesus calmly told them, "It is not the healthy who need a doctor, but the sick. I have not come to call the righteous, but sinners" (Mark 2:17 NIV). And how did He draw those sinners to Himself? By His love, His care for them, His compassion for their brokenness. He was Love incarnate, manifesting the tenderness of God to those in need of redemption. As we walk and live and build our lives, we are called to follow His example.

Love Defined

What is love, anyway? Many have asked but few seem to have a concrete definition. Yet the Master Blueprint is very clear on what love is. "Love is patient, love is kind. It does not envy, it does not boast, it is not proud. It is not rude, it is not self-seeking, it is not easily angered, it keeps no record of wrongs. Love does not delight in evil but rejoices with the truth. It always protects, always trusts, always hopes, always perseveres" (1 Cor. 13:4–7 NIV).

Love Is Patient

One translation states that "love suffers long" (1 Cor. 13:4 NKJV). When you love someone you go the distance even when the distance is painful. (Except in situations of abuse, of course. Then you should immediately leave the source and scene of danger.) But truly loving someone—anyone—will stretch you. You will have to extend more grace and mercy than you think you have. Love, like life, is not easy; it focuses more on giving than getting. It is selfless. This selflessness is what really empowers a person to rise above their humanity and love someone despite his or her weaknesses.

Take us, for instance: "God so loved the world that He gave His only begotten Son, that whosoever believes in Him should not perish but have everlasting life" (John 3:16 NKJV). Jesus' coming to Earth was all about what God ultimately wanted us to have. It wasn't just about God's wanting to claim us for His own; sacrificing His Son was about our having the greatest gift one could get—eternal life. God is completely selfless. I don't know if I would have been as gracious with a bunch of folks who didn't care about me! Would you?

As I consider the arguments of people who say that a loving God would not send people to hell, I have to respond, "Poppycock!" God is not "sending" anyone to hell. He has been waiting since time began for us to comprehend His love and embrace the way out—the way to heaven—that He makes available to everyone. He has given every person a fair choice. We get to choose where we go.

Since salvation is a free gift, no one has anything to lose; therefore we'd be crazy not to accept His offer. Thank God He is God and I am not. He offers more chances than I would. But that is because He is long-suffering. He does grieve over the lost. As a matter of fact, the only reason the end of time hasn't come yet is because He is "not willing that any man should perish but that all should come to repentance" (2 Pet. 3:9 NKJV). God keeps waiting and waiting, drawing out this whole thing called life to give all people a chance to have that amazing "aha" moment where they see His goodness and embrace it. How sweet is that?

Love Is Kind

That's the kindness of God, another attribute of love we should incorporate into the maintenance of our lives. It should color all we do. It is the goodness or kindness of God that drew us to Him and it is what draws others.

Love is the sealant of life; like a roof on a house, it covers all things, including "a multitude of sins" (1 Pet. 4:8 NASB). Small wonder in some translations *love* is called "charity" (KJV). The word *charity* implies giving without expecting anything back—simply giving because you have it to give and because you see a need you can fill. The reward comes from seeing the recipient transformed by your selflessness and love. You then find yourself energized because it always has been and always will be "more blessed to give than to receive" (Acts 20:35 NASB).

Love Does Not Envy or Boast, It Is Not Proud or Self-Seeking

If, however, we are envious, which comes from low self-esteem and insecurity, we become boastful and proud as a smoke screen. Many times we come off as just being plain ole rude and/or selfish. Of course these behaviors are contrary to love and can rupture all of our relationships. If you don't learn to master loving, your life can cave in! And selfish people—those who love with an ulterior motive—have a tendency to be easily offended.

Love Is Not Easily Angered

Another skill you must master in order for life to work is that of controlling anger. Being thin-skinned does not a happy life make. When you're touchy, you make everyone around you walk on eggshells to preserve the peace. And when someone does offend you, you usually wind up bitter because you nurse and rehearse the offense instead of letting it go.

> Life isn't all about you—not if you want to experience giving and receiving love.

How self-absorbed can you get? Life isn't all about you—not if you want to experience giving and receiving love.

Love Keeps No Record of Wrongs; Love Rejoices in the Truth

Love, in its truest form, does not assume the worst of other people or get happy when bad things happen to others. A person who loves doesn't keep track of other people's sins, and she seeks out the truth as well as a peaceful resolution in every conflict.

Love Protects, Trusts, Hopes, Endures

A loving person is protective of their relationships because he or she chooses to trust the beloved and hopes continually for the best in every relationship.

Believe it or not, God continually throws the things we do to offend Him into the sea of forgetfulness every time we truly repent. He is happy when we get things right. He always gives us the opportunity to do the right thing. He keeps hoping for the best in us and rooting for us to rise to our full potential and enjoy all the benefits of holy living (a holy life always works). Most touching of all, He never gives up on us.

To have lives that work, we are called and designed to be no less loving to others than He is to us.

When you love, you will always receive more than you give. But if you make yourself merely a recipient of love, you cut off love's momentum. To refuse to love is to destroy a life that works. This is the power of love: it is the true meaning of life and what really makes it work.

CONSTRUCTION TIP
"Love is as strong as death" (Song of Sol. 8:6), therefore, be careful where you place it and make sure the terms of exchange are always unconditional to ensure long life.

Long-Term Maintenance: Consistent Growth

The thing about life is, just as in home decorating, it's never done. There is never a stage where one stands back and says, "Okay, that's enough. I don't want to do anything more. I've seen it all—there's nothing else to discover or achieve." Well, unless you are just a hopeless couch potato, there will always be places to go, things to do, people to see, experiences to add to your life.

Everything in nature is designed to grow, to produce fruit. Jesus cursed a fig tree once for giving the illusion of having fruit to offer. It was in full bloom but bore no figs. He commanded it to wither and die (Matt. 21:18–19). It was useless, taking up space and pretending to be something that it was not.

Some people are like this fig tree. They walk through life appearing to have a lot to offer but up close, you find great pretenders. They bear no "fruit"—have nothing useful to give others—they're all show and no substance. A lack of productivity and the refusal to mature will stymie a life that is working—and it won't work for long.

God wants us moving forward, being productive, maturing from the challenges we face. We then have "fruit" to share—the life lessons we pick up along the way. When we pass on these lessons, we empower others to grow and be fruitful as well. This is the cycle of life. We cross-pollinate!

Self-Assessment

In order to keep growing, you'll sometimes need to check out where you are to get an idea of where you need to go. If you're not sure how to go about self-examination, ask some people you respect—close friends, mentors, pastors—what areas they think you could grow in. Find people able and willing to give you an honest appraisal of your life.

When looking for people to help you evaluate and grow, consider those who are mature, well seasoned, and successful in the areas in which you would like to succeed. Don't overlook those who are significantly older than yourself. We live in a society that glamorizes youth and discards the elderly. They are no longer appreciated or considered precious. These people have seen more of life than you and I. If they've kept learning and growing, they have had long lives that work, and they have much to share.

This might be difficult to do at first, but simply ask the person you select:

- ✳ What area do you think I've grown the most in?
- ✳ Where do you think I need to grow more?
- ✳ What indicates to you that I need more growth in this area?
- ✳ What types of things would you suggest I consider?

The hard part for you will be not to get defensive, no matter what they say. Remember you are talking to someone you love and trust. Weigh what he or she says, find the truth in it, and build on it.

The bottom line is, make plans to grow—don't leave this function to chance. Life is ever unfolding. When you stop growing, you start stagnating.

Life nurtures life. The more you know, the more you have to offer others. Rich fruit is borne from constant learning and maturing. Then, when others partake of your life, they are blessed by it. In all we do, we are aiming for the fruit that comes from maturity and allowing God to perfect us as we go through the seasons of our lives. We should flourish and abound in fruitfulness and every good work.

Our lives are continually under construction until we grow up to the measure of the stature of the fullness of Christ. At that point we will be our most fruitful. Maturity has everything do with our productivity. This is why the Blueprint instructs us to be perfect (or mature) as the One who designed us is perfect (Matt. 5:48). We are to look just like Him. Yet many resist growing because it is not the most comfortable process.

What Happens When We Refuse to Grow

To borrow a biblical analogy, as branches grafted into the true Vine, Christ Jesus, we must occasionally be pruned. He said, "I am the true vine, and my Father is the gardener. He cuts off every branch in me that bears no fruit, while every branch that does bear fruit he prunes so that it will be even more fruitful" (John 15:1–2 NIV). The things that impede our progress must be cleared away in order for healthy growth to take place.

When the Master Architect (the Gardener) performs this pruning, many feel as if their faith is like hugging a knife: it's painful to hold on to but it's too dangerous to let go. Sometimes God has to exercise severe mercy by moving in spite of us to save us from ourselves or those things that will damage the fruit we are yet to bear.

When we truly understand the design of the Architect—our ultimate growth and prosperity of spirit—we open our hands and let go, allowing Him to take out what He must and give us what He wants.

Many of us rob ourselves of the opportunity to experience God's best for our lives.

I once attempted to spring-clean my house and made up my mind to really get rid of some things. But each thing I picked up had some sentimental value and I found myself putting it right back where I found it. At the end of the day, my load was no lighter, my space no clearer. What I didn't realize then is that not cleaning (self-pruning) leaves no room for new things, better things, no room for God to surprise me. It is only when I am willing to get rid of the old that the opportunity for new things presents itself. Like a woman holding on to a bad man because she believes something is better than nothing, many of us rob ourselves of the opportunity to experience God's best for our lives.

What Maturity Is All About

Mature people, people who consistently choose to grow, are able to honestly assess when a season is over and welcome change and a new season. They see the value of the process and embrace it wholeheartedly. They put away childish things and rationalizations with no lingering sentiment or regret. They look forward to standing complete in the will of God, fully fruitful.

Maturity is not for the faint of heart or for those who don't have a stomach for the solid things of God. "Solid food is for the mature, who by constant use have trained themselves to distinguish good from evil" (Heb. 5:14 NIV). Mature people not only recognize good and evil, they make right choices. As you mature, you should be making fewer bad decisions.

Maturity takes a lifetime to master but it is possible. The Master Architect just keeps adjusting us, stretching us, tearing down and building up, but the apostle Peter tells us: "After you have suffered a little while, [He] will himself restore you and make you strong, firm and steadfast" (1 Pet. 5:10 NIV). We will then be perfect buildings constructed for His glory.

Established, you finally know who you are and what you have to offer. You are free to celebrate and encourage others without feeling the need to compete for accolades. Strengthened, you have grown physical and spiritual muscles that make you strong enough to walk through the storms and trials of life without being bowed over by them. You, like the apostle Paul, who suffered many hardships for the sake of the gospel, will be able to say at the end of the day, "I have fought a good fight, I have finished the course, I have kept the faith" (2 Tim. 4:7 NIV).

Participating in the growth that leads to maturity makes you steadfast, unwavering, and focused. Keeping your eye on the prize, you keep moving forward—keep growing—no matter what is going on because you've established some things in your heart and your soul, and you'll never turn away or aside. You will be settled, and like a building firmly entrenched in its foundation, you will not be moved by calamity.

Others will be able to enter in and partake of all the richness that comes from the fullness of your character. They can feed from your wisdom, draw comfort from your peace, be restored by your joy, calmed by your gentleness, fed by your goodness. Shall I go on?

If you are currently in the pruning process—struggling through a rough season—remember that you are not alone in the struggle.

Those who wait upon the LORD
Shall renew their strength;

They shall mount up with wings like eagles,
They shall run and not be weary,
They shall walk and not faint. (Isaiah 40:31 NKJV)

Those who keep growing enjoy life on a whole other level because of all that they have endured and learned, free to soar above all the circumstances that will present themselves in the course of life. Without this, life will not keep working.

CONSTRUCTION TIP
It is only through growth that the quality of our lives can be established and sound. Each life is uniquely equipped to bear its own brand of fruit.

Accessories

- ✳ Righteousness
- ✳ Peace
- ✳ Joy
- ✳ Favor and Blessing
- ✳ Invaluable Intangibles
- ✳ Honor

Accessories: Spare No Expense

Accessories are a must. Accessories vary in price, depending on their value. You can pick and choose which ones you want and ignore those not important to you. Though others might have the same accessories you do, they may utilize them differently.

Accessories beautify things and add the finishing touch to all that is essential in your world. Therefore choose wisely; spare no expense to get the ones that will add life and that extra *je ne sais quoi* to what you already have. The accessories of your life should not only be attractive, they should be contagious—that is, others celebrate their beauty and want what you have. That is when you know that you've chosen well and that the cost was worth it.

Righteousness

S trangely enough, not everyone chooses to obtain righteousness, even though the Master Architect Himself purchased it for us all. It's always available, but you must use your God-given voucher to receive it. This is highly recommended, as many features of your working life will not operate well without it.

The voucher is Jesus Christ, the Son of God. He said, "I am the way, and the truth, and the life; no one comes to the Father but through Me" (John 14:6 NASB). He paid the price to have your previous fixture, your sin nature, washed away so you could have access to the Father, the Master Architect, and free entry into His kingdom. Though God wants to use us to reach others for Himself, the first person you need to be concerned about is you. Are you right with God?

This is a question that can be settled only between you and your Maker. If you've never obtained this accessory, now is as good a time as any to do so. Note that this righteousness cannot be earned. It is a free gift from God and cannot be attached to any good works, so no one can take the credit for being righteous in himself (Eph. 2:8–9). We can partake of the righteousness of God only through Christ Jesus (Rom. 3:22), who paid the penalty for our sin nature so that the enemy of our souls can no longer disqualify us from gaining entrance into the presence of God.

If you've never accepted the gift of Christ's righteousness, take a moment to pray this very simple prayer from the depths of your heart.

> Dear Heavenly Father, I want to be in right standing with You. I want to be Your child. I want access to all You have for me. I confess that I am a sinner in need of Your salvation. Please forgive me and cleanse me of my sin, wash me and make me whole. Lord Jesus, I ask You to come into my heart. Be my Lord and Savior. Teach me Your ways that I might reflect your grace and glorify You in all I say and do.
>
> This day I decree that I am a new creature in Christ. Seal me unto the day of redemption. Keep me and teach me by Your Spirit from this day forward. In Jesus' name, amen.

You, my friend, have just cashed in on the priceless gift of righteousness.

The Perks and Privileges at Your Disposal

This accessory comes with major perks and privileges. Let's take a look.

Access to God

After we are made right with God, have "right standing" with Him, we have access to Him in prayer with the guarantee that He will hear and answer us, and we have the promise of eternal life while enjoying the privileges of "kingdom living" right here on Earth. Righteousness, peace, and joy in the Holy Ghost are the full essence of kingdom living. The peace that comes from knowing all is well between you and your Maker should fill you with joy (more on these two features later).

Access to God's Power and Protection

This right standing with God also means that He will come to your defense. "When a man's ways are pleasing the LORD, He makes even his enemies to be at peace with him" (Prov. 16:7 NASB). He will be your Protector, your Provider, your Counselor—everything you need in order for life to work for you. This takes a huge burden off of you!

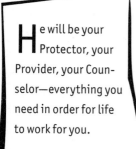

He will be your Protector, your Provider, your Counselor—everything you need in order for life to work for you.

You have become a partner with God. He will assist you in living your best life and when you have done everything—exerted all your energy and know-how—"you can stand and see the salvation of the LORD on your behalf" (2 Chron. 20:17 NASB). Though you cannot shirk your own responsibility to make decisions and follow the Blueprint, the Master Architect will assist and empower you.

Access to God's Resources

Because you are a partner with Him, His vast and endless resources are yours as well. You have become a joint heir with His Son, Jesus Christ: "As many as received Him [Christ], to them He gave the right to become children of God, to those who believe in His name" (John 1:12 NKJV). When you are part of a family, you have access to everything belonging to your family. You can now "approach the throne of grace with confidence, so that [you] may receive mercy and find grace to help [you] in [your] time of need" (Heb. 4:16 NIV).

※

Righteousness is a precious accessory and should become a permanent fixture. Many do not recognize its eternal value until it is too late. Some, upon finally acquiring it, wish they had taken hold of it sooner. You can't appreciate its true value and beauty until you've added it to your life, but once you do you will never suffer from buyer's remorse. The guarantee that comes with righteousness is worth its weight in gold alone: "The wicked are overthrown and are no more, but the house of the righteous will stand" (Prov. 12:7 NASB). And life works a lot better when your house is standing.

Peace

The peace that comes from knowing God is a priceless accessory. His peace, unlike the fragile, temporary kind the world has, is deep and immovable; it should keep us from being anxious or afraid. His peace gives completeness, tranquility, soundness of mind and heart, and a consistent feeling of great safety. It is an accessory only the Architect can give (John 14:27).

This accessory comes with instructions on how to use it. It is important to know that "the mind controlled by the Spirit is life and peace" (Rom. 8:6 NIV), therefore we have to "make every effort to do what leads to peace and to mutual edification" (Rom. 14:19 NIV). How do we do that? Well, first we very consciously make the decision to trust God in all matters. If we truly know and love Him, then we also trust Him and know that He not only knows what is best for us, He *wants* what is best for us.

And because, as the Blueprint tells us, we know "all things work together for the good of those who love God, to those who are the called according to His purpose" (Rom. 8:28 NKJV), we can trust that no matter what our situation is, it will work out for good.

When writing to the Philippian church, the great apostle Paul told them (and us):

Do not be anxious about anything, but in everything, by prayer and petition, with thanksgiving, present your requests to God. And the peace of God, which transcends all understanding, will guard your hearts and your minds in Christ Jesus.... Whatever you have learned or received or heard from me, or seen in me—put it into practice. And the God of peace will be with you. (Philippians 4:6–7, 9 NIV)

Use Peace as a Discernment Tool

Sometimes a lack of peace can be a good thing. If you've made a decision but don't have peace about it, that is a sign to pray and get clarity from God. The issue could be a matter of timing, the people involved, or the entire decision. Again, you should never move forward on a decision for which you lack peace. Find out what's wrong and fix it.

When God smiles on a situation, perfect peace will accompany you as you move forward. Do not let time constraints cost you your discernment. You should never be in a hurry; the right move at the wrong time can be just as costly as the wrong move at any time.

The Blueprint promises, "You will keep him in perfect peace whose mind is stayed on You, because he trusts in You" (Isa. 26:3 NKJV). Staying our minds on God means we constantly check in with Him and reflect on His goodness and His ability to guide us and keep us. Our trust in Him gives us peace as we face everyday issues knowing He has our backs.

> When God smiles on a situation, perfect peace will accompany you as you move forward.

Not for Sale

The reality of life is that you can't buy peace—can't bottle it, can't get it on your own. All counterfeit forms of peace will not last because the only source of true peace is Jesus (Eph. 2:14). Without Him, the Prince of Peace, we can't have perfect peace because we are at war with God.

This is why it is important to know that guilt is a function not of the intellect but of the Spirit. When the Spirit comes calling you as God called Adam, saying, "Where are you?" own your stuff. Say, "Here am I, Lord, in need of cleansing. Set me free from the bondage of my own bad choices and sin." Jesus died for moments like this— when the price He paid on Calvary can kick in to restore you to your right place before God, creating reconciliation and freedom from the disease of guilt. Trust me, confession before a gracious God is a powerful thing.

The choice is yours. You can let the peace of God rule in your heart and keep you or try to fight the good fight alone. I suggest you add this accessory to your shopping cart immediately and get on with the business of life.

Joy

J oy is a beautiful accessory. It is all things light and beautiful. Everyone is attracted to it. Ever found yourself laughing because someone else was laughing? Joy is the release you feel at the end of anything that causes tension. It is the break, the comma in the middle of the sentence that supplies the breath we need to finish. We don't just want joy. We *need* joy.

Let us not mistake joy for happiness. Let's clarify: Happiness is an external feature that is regulated by outward stimuli. It can occur at any given time and fluctuate wildly based on changing conditions. Joy, however, is internal and will not be manipulated by people or circumstances.

David wrote, "In Your presence is fullness of joy; in Your right hand there are pleasures forever" (Ps. 16:11 NASB). Basking in the presence of God gives you a joy that becomes contagious to everyone around you. You should look like the cat that ate the canary to your peers, friends, and family because of the time you spend with God. When you live according to the Blueprint, you feel His favor in every area of your life. This increases your joy because your prayers are being answered and you are experiencing God's goodness.

Unfortunately, many don't buy the entire joy accessory kit because the prerequisite for experiencing such fullness of joy is tears. "Those who sow in tears shall reap in joy" (Ps. 126:5 NKJV). It is almost impossible to appreciate joy without tears. It is almost as if the tears wash away some things, clearing the deck for the joy that is to follow. In God's grace we find life: "Weeping may endure for a night, but joy comes in the morning" (Ps. 30:5 NKJV). Sometimes the night season lasts for a while, but when the sun finally rises, chasing away the shadows of your trial, the brightness is astounding. In those moments your joy is pure. It is relief. It is thankfulness for answered prayer. It is full.

Where Can I Get Some?

Where does this joy that we all long for come from? Perhaps this is the key to why so many fail to find it. Joy is not found in the accumulation of possessions, the accolades of men, the breadth of our achievements, or even in the love of our dreams. True joy comes from...

The Lord
He is the source of all joy. He created it and now imparts it to you by His Spirit. When He comes to abide in your heart—when you accept His righteousness—He brings all of His attributes with Him. His presence in your life ensures that you will always have everything He has, including His joy.

The Word (Blueprint)
Knowing His Word and all of the promises He has made to you, including that your salvation is secure, brings "glorious, inexpressible joy" (1 Pet. 1:8). When you know what you are entitled to, you have confidence, and confidence gives you joy unspeakable.

Having full knowledge of your spiritual rights and the benefits that being a child of God affords you should make you feel like a very wealthy heir, a member of a very prominent and important family.

Knowing that God not only gives you His Word but also stands behind it—because He cannot lie or backtrack from His Word—should further bolster your joy because you don't have to question your relationship or His intentions toward you. You don't have to wonder if He will do what He says He will do.

God's Promises

Let's look at what the Blueprint says about the promises of God.

- ❊ Praise the LORD who has given rest to his people Israel, just as he promised. Not one word has failed of all the wonderful promises he gave through his servant Moses. (1 Kings 8:56)
- ❊ Your promises have been thoroughly tested; that is why I love them so much. (Psalm 199:140)
- ❊ By that same mighty power, he has given us all of his rich and wonderful promises. He has promised that you will escape the decadence all around you caused by evil desires and that you will share in his divine nature. (2 Peter 1:4)

You can have confidence that God has given you victory over your enemies: "You prepare a feast for me in the presence of my enemies" (Ps. 23:5). He promises to completely vindicate you: "Commit everything you do to the LORD. Trust him, and he will help you. He will make your innocence as clear as the dawn, and the justice of your cause will shine like the noonday sun" (Ps. 37:5–6). This should make your heart glad when others offend or falsely accuse you. You don't have to worry because God

You don't have to worry because God Himself has your back.

Himself has your back. He sees all and intervenes, taking up the causes of those who have been wronged.

You can rejoice because you know your labor is never wasted: "Be strong and steady, always enthusiastic about the Lord's work, for you know that nothing you do for the Lord is ever useless" (1 Cor. 15:58). It is always a joyous occasion when God grants us increase. All of our hard work and tears have paid off, not just materially, but in the nurturing of dreams and aspirations.

There is much to celebrate in life. Rehearsing all of the blessings of God and His many benefits keeps you in the right frame of mind to be open to even more blessings than you can imagine.

These are the things that make God happy. He loves us. He loves having us in His presence and seeing us triumph over every aspect of life. The things that give Him joy actually strengthen us. Yes, the joy of the Lord is our strength (Neh. 8:10)! His joy gives us joy. It feeds us and fills us with gladness.

This accessory is a natural part of a life that works.

Favor and Blessing

When you find favor with someone, you gain his approval, acceptance, or special benefits and blessings because of how he feels about you. This accessory may seem like mere decoration but it is necessary in the décor of your life. You can't get far without favor. Think about how we often need a recommendation to get a job—a good word spoken to get us into a group or organization. Someone who can testify as to why you add something valuable to the mix can make all the difference.

Favor opens doors. Favor and blessing have everything to do with how and when God regards you. Sometimes in the Bible, what He saw in the lives of those He wanted to bless made Him turn His face away. Samson is a good example.

As I've mentioned, Samson wasted his strength and anointing on women while his countrymen strained under the bondage of their enemies. He preferred to spend his time reveling in the things that appealed to his flesh rather than walking in his calling to begin the deliverance of his people from the Philistines. His dalliances with the wrong women finally led him to his ruin—quite to his surprise. He took the presence and protection of God along with his own strength for granted until that fateful evening when his enemies descended upon him to take him captive.

When He looks at us, blessing is in His gaze.

The story goes that when Delilah warned that the Philistines were at hand, "He awoke from his sleep and thought, 'I'll go out as before and shake myself free.' But he did not know that the Lord had left him" (Judg. 16:20 NIV). The rest is history. He was bound, blinded, and taken into bondage. He died making one last effort to wreak vengeance on the Philistines. How much more he could have done if he had spent more time making God smile than he did pleasing himself.

This is never a good thing. When God turns His face away, it leaves you open for anything to come against—and triumph over—you.

Through Moses, God blessed the people of Israel, saying, "The LORD bless and keep you; the LORD make His face shine upon you, and be gracious to you" (Num. 6:24–25 NKJV). Solomon wrote, "In the light of the king's face is life" (Prov. 16:15 NKJV). When He looks at us, blessing is in His gaze, but when He looks away we find that the disregard of God is a lonely and unfruitful place to dwell.

When Jesus became sin for us on the cross and God looked away, it was the most painful moment of Jesus' life, more painful than the scourging and the nails in His hands and feet. That moment of separation must have felt like an unbearable eternity. Small wonder David cried out in a psalm, "Do not cast me away from Your presence and do not take Your Holy Spirit from me" (Ps. 51:11 NASB)! Separation from God is not something you want to experience once you've known the joy of fellowship and deep intimacy with Him.

Who Gets Blessed?

So whom does God choose to bless with His favor and why? Basically, those who walk in righteousness: "It is You who blesses the righteous man, O LORD, You surround him with favor as with a shield" (Ps. 5:12 NASB). Such people call out to God, "Let the favor of the LORD our God be upon us; and confirm for us the work of our hands" (Ps. 90:17 NASB).

And when God decides to bless you, it's all good: "It is the blessing of the LORD that makes rich, and He adds no sorrow to it" (Prov. 10:22 NASB). In some instances when you acquire some things, they add more drama to your life than you bargained for. But when God blesses you, nothing is attached but blessing. When God blesses you, you will be able to enjoy it without the extra burden of "fine print" that can sometimes take the joy out of the acquisition.

Benefits of Favor

More Influence
God's blessings cause you to be fruitful and increase, not just in gain but in influence because others see the goodness of God operating in your life and glorify Him.

This was the case with Daniel, a wonderful man of God and prayer warrior. Some of his peers were jealous of Daniel's favor with the king and sought to get him in trouble (Dan. 6). They manipulated the king into declaring that the people could pray to no one but King Darius himself. Daniel, a man of God, prayed only to God. When, as punishment, he was thrown in a lions' den to be devoured, the favor of God covered him. That night an angel protected Daniel.

King Darius was so impressed, he commanded the people to worship Daniel's God!

That is the type of life that God wants us all to lead—one with the reputation of being blessed by the favor of God. Again, when we curry favor and a good name with God, we can also gain these things in the sight of men:

> Let your heart keep my commandments;
> For length of days and years of life
> And peace they will add to you.
> Do not let kindness and truth leave you;
> Bind them around your neck,
> Write them on the tablet of your heart.
> So you will find favor and good report
> In the sight of God and man. (Proverbs 3:1–4 NASB)

Power to Bless

A good reputation also places us in a position to favor others. Remember that we are blessed in order to be a blessing to others. When favor is at work in your life, you can go places others can't, do what others can't, and say what others could never get away with. This is because you know you are walking under the cloud cover of God's favor and you are moving as He directs you.

One day I was in Beverly Hills with friends, and we passed a very famous, posh restaurant. I decided I wanted to have lunch there to see all the stars. My friends chided that I did not have a reservation and it would be impossible to get in. My response was to remind them I had the favor of God on my life, saunter up to the maitre d', and request a table for four for McKinney Hammond.

The host looked at his reservation list. Of course I was not there. He asked me to repeat my request, which I calmly did. He looked at his list again, then showed us to a table! As we were ordering dessert, he again came to confirm my name and made sure we had enjoyed our meal. We had a good laugh. I finally got enough breath to say, "Sometimes you just have to act as if you belong where you want to go and leave the rest up to God's favor to open the doors!"

This is a lighthearted example, but the favor of God will open doors for you and promote you in the sight of many. In short, these two accessories, favor and blessing, make for a very exciting life. How long does His favor last? "His anger is but for a moment, His favor for a lifetime" (Ps. 30:5 NASB). These are accessories you really can't do without in a life that works! Favor and blessing are life-enhancement accessories. They make you look special. They set you apart from the rest.

Warning: Allow the favor of God, not your own insistence, to open doors for you. God's favor will always bring the best results.

Invaluable Intangibles

Many work hard to store up all sorts of *things* and find themselves unable to enjoy them for various reasons. Many have much in terms of "stuff," but their riches have become the bane of their existence, surrounding them in scandal, intense scrutiny, unwelcome criticism, and the ever-present paparazzi. These things leave you feeling bankrupt though your bank statement might show you have plenty of actual cash.

In order to enjoy this wonderful accessory in a way that works well with your life, you first need to understand what true wealth is. I've said this before, but let me affirm: wealth is much more than material possessions. It is the intangibles, the things you cannot buy, such as health—mental, physical, and spiritual—and rich relationships with true friends who don't abandon you when trouble hits but stand and believe and pray with you until you pull through, providing whatever tangible help they can. No amount of money can secure these things for you. They are gifts from God often maintained by making the right choices for yourself along the journey of life.

> Wealth reaches far beyond material trappings to the things that really matter to our hearts.

It's the simple things that seem to be the most complicated to obtain—the things that enrich life and make one feel truly wealthy regardless of financial status. Many poor people are unaware that they are poor because their lives are so rich. Wealth reaches far beyond material trappings to the things that really matter to our hearts.

How to Get the Invaluable Intangibles

How do we get this enduring wealth? By seeking God and wisdom. We looked at Proverbs 10:22 in the last chapter: "The blessing of the LORD brings wealth, and he adds no trouble to it" (*The Message*). It is God who gives you the power to gain anything of value, and wisdom gives you the power to keep it.

This is yet another accessory that earmarks you in a crowd. A person who has gained great love and loyalty, who enjoys God's blessing emotionally and spiritually, stands out because he or she is so happy! Others will notice the difference, though they might not be able to verbalize it. Righteousness speaks for itself. As the psalmist put it:

The generation of the upright will be blessed.
Wealth and riches are in his house,
    and his righteousness endures forever.
Even in darkness light dawns for the upright,
    for the gracious and compassionate and righteous man.
Good will come to him who is generous and lends freely,
    who conducts his affairs with justice.
Surely he will never be shaken;
    a righteous man will be remembered forever.

He will have no fear of bad news;
    his heart is steadfast, trusting in the LORD.
His heart is secure, he will have no fear;
    in the end he will look in triumph on his foes.
He has scattered abroad his gifts to the poor,
    his righteousness endures forever;
his horn will be lifted high in honor. (Psalm 112:2–9 NIV)

This is the essence of true wealth and prosperity as distinguished from simply amassed riches. It is a life that is well balanced in its gain, one that is flourishing and fruitful, spiritually and naturally. You are in good physical health, you are mentally sound, your relationships are working, your career is progressing, your reputation is sterling, you are walking in favor, and others around you are the better for spending time in your presence. It is a life well spent.

Spread Out the Blessings

A person blessed with the invaluable intangibles pursues not just what would bless them but what would bless others. This is what you do when you prosper: you get to a place of rest in all of your affairs and this releases you to be generous.

This is the stuff legacies are made of. It is said that "a good man leaves an inheritance for his children's children" (Prov. 13:22 NIV). Again, this inheritance is of more than material things. Just as sin can visit up to the fourth generation in a family, righteousness, good character, and good works can spread from parent to child to grandchild and beyond. Every day you get to create a legacy for the next generation by the way you live out your life—how you spend your time as well as your money.

※

ULTIMATELY, AT THE culmination of your days, your soul should be well satisfied as it surveys this precious accessory—the things no money can buy—that will beautify the lives of many.

Honor

This accessory is hard to locate. It will not be found in the obvious place, sitting out front and center on anyone's hardware rack. Though everyone wants honor, it is difficult to come by because the route one must take to get it is not a preferred path. The world teaches that we must all strive to get to the top, make things happen. We are taught to build our own kingdoms and seek our own honor. Yet in God's kingdom quite the reverse is true. According to the Manufacturer's Blueprint, humility is the prerequisite to honor (Prov. 15:33). It seems that in the kingdom, the way up is down.

Consequently, all you've ever learned about gaining promotion must be reversed. And humility and fear of the Lord can bring not only honor but wealth and long life (Prov. 22:4)! If we pursue righteousness and love, it is likely that in our search we will also find life, prosperity, and honor (Prov. 21:21).

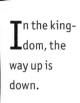

In the kingdom, the way up is down.

Sounds simple, but can we really pull it off? Because we struggle with *doing* rather than *being*, the lines get blurred. It is hard to resist the urge to make things happen—to work up a crowd reaction and get everyone standing up and proclaiming your greatness. But let's face it: tooting our own horns can come off as acting unjustifiably grandiose and lead to great embarrassment. And so we are discouraged from seeking our own honor.

The Only Way to True Honor

The Blueprint tells us that those who exalt themselves will be humbled and those who humble themselves will be exalted (Luke 14:8–11). The best way to gain honor is to humble yourself—then the Lord can lift you up.

> Serve each other in humility, for
>
> > "God sets himself against the proud,
> > but he shows favor to the humble."
>
> So humble yourselves under the mighty power of God, and in his good time he will honor you. (1 Peter 5:5–6)

Any honor we seek should be for the sake of giving the honor back to the One who truly deserves it—that would be God. Without Him we would have and be nothing.

The Only Source of True Honor

Honor is an interesting accessory because it cannot be bought; it has to be earned. Once acquired, it is a thing of great beauty. And yet you cannot earn it on your own. Understand that promotion comes from the Lord:

> I warned the proud, "Stop your boasting!"
> I told the wicked, "Don't raise your fists!

Don't lift your fists in defiance at the heavens
　　or speak with rebellious arrogance."
For no one on earth—from east or west,
　　or even from the wilderness—
Can raise another person up.
　　It is God alone who judges;
he decides who will rise and will fall. (Psalm 75:4–7)

Honor is established by the moving of God's Spirit on your behalf. "It is not by force nor by strength, but by my Spirit, says the LORD Almighty" (Zech. 4:6). He accomplishes it all so that you can in no way take credit for the glory of it all.

An Example of Power Gone Wrong

Greed for honor and power were what got Satan in trouble (Ezek. 28). He was a favored son until the day a root of iniquity was found in his heart. Like a fine splinter, this little root of unwarranted pride irritated him until he acted upon his treacherous thoughts. He felt that he deserved just as much honor and glory as God because of his great beauty. Why not grab some praise and worship for himself?

Leading a third of the heavenly hosts in rebellion, Satan's coup was quickly circumvented by the Lamb of God, Jesus Himself. Satan and his naïve minions were hurled out of heaven and forever out of the presence and favor of God. To this day they are still awaiting their eternal punishment, which will be administered at the end of ages.

What a demotion! So much for grabbing the honor for yourself. It just won't happen, or at best it will be short-lived.

Though Satan was demoted, his influence is alive and well. Many seeking the esteem of men are still deceived that this is something they can secure for themselves. The media would convince us that many have achieved this without any help from God. But there is a difference between what God allows and what He ordains. Any gain you create for yourself will be temporal, have no lasting value. Only what we do for Christ will last. Only what God gifts you with will remain eternally and not rot or suffer a short shelf life. It will last forever (Luke 12:32–33).

Honor is no more than decoration if it doesn't come from God. In a life that works, honor must be a secure accessory, not just eye candy. Jesus made it clear that in His eyes life is more than food, raiment, or the accolades of men (Luke 12:23)—all temporary things. Only what lasts is worth pursuing. "What will last?" you ask. The good works God records in heaven on your account. Make pleasing God your mission. Look at what He promised the Israelites through Moses:

> It shall come to pass, if you diligently obey the voice of the LORD your God, to observe carefully all His commandments which I command you today, that the LORD your God will set you high above all nations of the earth. And all these blessings will come upon you and overtake you, because you obey the voice of the LORD your God.... And the LORD will make you the head and not the tail; you shall be above only, and not be beneath, if you heed the commandments of the LORD your God, which I command you today, and are careful to observe them. (Deuteronomy 28:1–2, 13 NKJV)

Honor will become the residual effect of all those blessings.

Here again you receive what you give. Honor is an attitude of respect, courtesy, and reverence. As we give honor to God through our reverence and obedience, "the LORD will give grace and glory; no good thing will He withhold from those who walk uprightly" (Ps. 84:11 NKJV). In this way every blessing you receive is yet another opportunity to give honor to whom honor is due. Funny thing about honor—once you have it you can't help but give it away in order to accessorize the lives of others.

Troubleshooting

※ When life caves in...

※ When life won't work...

※ When life gets stuck...

※ When life seems
uncertain...

※ When life seems over...

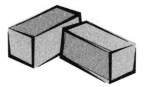

When life caves in . . .

As I began to write this book, everything in my life went crazy. My business collapsed, I lost valued employees, my finances imploded and bottomed out, my health took a downward spiral, I fell into a deep depression, I couldn't concentrate to write, friends died, and even my dog got sick! At one point I put my hands over my head and just shouted, "Stop the madness!"

All of this to say: I know of what I speak.

What do you do when you find yourself like Job, sitting in the middle of the complete mess called your life without any explanation for why the whirlwind occurred and left nothing standing? Do you take Job's wife's suggestion and curse God and die? Do you pull a Mr. Magoo? (Remember him? He was nearsighted and he walked through life completely unaware of the devastation going on around him.)

There's something to be said for just moving forward no matter what is going on. If you can keep putting one foot in front of the other, you will eventually reach the end of your trial. We've been assured that weeping lasts for a night but joy comes in the morning. This is just a test. So what do you do in the meantime?

First, understand that nothing stays the same, so decide not to lie down just because everything is falling down. Decide to keep going no matter what. (See the section on Perseverance for further help.)

Next, search for the lesson in the trial. There's always something to learn. Remember that pain is an indicator that something is wrong. Don't run from it; embrace it and let it talk to you.

Continue to trust God. He is not out to get you and He is not cruelly experimenting with your life. Like a determined parent, He is cheering you on to greater growth so that you can be mature enough to handle all the things He wants to give you. But He will give them only when He can trust you to handle them.

Nurture a grateful heart in spite of your circumstances and don't give in to complaining and negative confessions. Say things that will produce good fruit.

Surround yourself with a good support system. Don't let pride make you secretive about your struggles. That can only hurt you. Share what you are going through with trustworthy friends who can give sound and loving counsel.

Last but certainly not least, stay prayerful and open to God's instruction. Be in tune with His timing, recognize the season you are in, yield to the changes, and anticipate and prepare for the next phase of life. How and when you get to move on depends on how you respond to where you are right now.

As for me, eventually I finished my book, as you can see since you are reading it. I could not give in to how I was feeling; my public awaited and my passion to share life-giving information drove me to the finish line. I was late but at least I finished.

As for the rest of my life, well, I'm rebuilding it one brick at a time. As I sorted through the rubble I found some things that needed to be thrown away and others worthy of keeping. Perhaps if a complete dismantling had not taken place I wouldn't have noticed.

When everything stays the same, nothing changes. That may sound redundant to you, but it really isn't. In order to move forward or take life to the next level, some things have to be removed because they will impede your progress. This usually reveals itself only in the midst of a shake-up. The Master Architect knows this and proclaims that

He is shaking everything that can be shaken so that only what is eternal will remain (Heb. 12:27). So when there is a whole lot of shakin' goin' on, celebrate—and get ready for the renovations!

> [He] redeems your life from the pit
> and crowns you with love and compassion.
> —Psalm 103:4 NIV

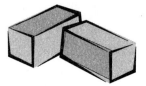

When life won't work...

A fter listening to his guests waxing eloquent about how they're dealing with a certain critical issue, a famous talk show host frequently asks, "How's that working for you?" The test of whether you're on the right track is if you see your efforts producing good results. Sometimes in life it can seem as if nothing is happening because all the work and changes are being done beneath the surface. But at some point in time, evidence of the underground activity will come to light.

Your life was designed to be fruitful, productive, effective, joyful, and fulfilling. If any or all of these ingredients are missing, it's time to find out why. This usually requires exploring below the surface to see what's broken.

First, admit that life is not working. God cannot and will not fix what you won't admit.

Next, check your foundation. Are the cornerstones in perfect alignment? How about the God Cornerstone (the most important of the four)? Perhaps you need to shorten the distance between the You Cornerstone and the God Cornerstone. Draw closer. Draw close enough to hear what He is saying. Sometimes we don't want to hear what God has to say because we are afraid of what He might require of us. And yet whatever He speaks gives life. When we listen and obey, life will work for us.

If the You and the God Cornerstones are okay, how is the Others Cornerstone? Have you been suffering through love relationships that start great but always implode? Are you falling into repeated conflicts with coworkers? Look for patterns of behavior that may be sabotaging your good intentions. This will be your key to discovering the problem.

We've all heard it said that if you want something different to happen, you have to *do* something different. Change your approach in order to make relationships run smoother and last longer. That's right, flip the script on your attitude, words, and actions. This is within your power.

Check also the Purpose Cornerstone. Are you working in conjunction with what God made you to do—or are you stubbornly trying to fit a different mold?

Seek God and good friends for counsel. Accept direction. No one has all the answers. Start where you can and build on what you can secure. If you are faithful with the little things, you will eventually be trusted with more. Remain steady and consistent.

Stay sensitive to when things need to change. This one is huge. Sometimes we settle into something—a habit, a job, a relationship— that worked well for a space of time but now is destructive to our lives. Know when it's time to let go, leave, or change the channel! Don't wait until things stop working altogether. Get a jump start on repairing and salvaging anything worth saving and get rid of the rest before it becomes a major hindrance.

Last, realign your perspective. Sometimes life is working, *just not according to your design.* Then you need to refocus and find out what God wants your life to look like. If you are not following the Architect's Blueprint, it simply won't stand strong or last. Somewhere along the way the construction will have to come to a complete stop because there is no clear direction.

When everything crashes at once, it's time to recheck the original design. Repent, if need be, of taking your life in your own hands and get back on track. Take it one day at a time. Keep the faith, persist, and life will be back up and running in no time.

> Hold on to instruction, do not let it go;
> guard it well, for it is your life.
> —Proverbs 4:13 NIV

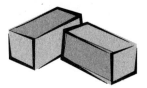

When life gets stuck...

D ead ends—gotta love 'em. They signal that you can go no farther. Your only choice is to turn around and go back the way you came, keeping your eye open for a better route to get where you want to go.

Getting stuck in a rut is a signal that it is time to change direction—to take life up a notch. It may be time to broaden your influence. It's almost always time to give more, serve more, love more, live more. Whenever people complain about being bored, their complaints reveal that they are *boring*. They are not doing enough to stimulate themselves or others. Take the time to assess the areas of sameness in your life and evaluate how you can capitalize on what you have already been doing and take it to another level.

Growth demands that we keep adding to what already exists. Life will not allow us to stay comfortable. Therefore we begin to experience discomfort and unrest. It is the Spirit within trying to show us we can do so much more. We should never be content to drift. If we are, we will eventually reach a dead end and have to take action.

As I said earlier, consistent growth is part of your long-term maintenance program. If you settle at a dead end, you will experience dry rot. Growing is healthy. The Master Architect is always at work. When we resist checking the floor plan, we eventually hit a wall where He was ready to create a passageway to somewhere extraordinary. He is always doing a new thing, improving on the design of your life, but you must look up in order to see where He is leading and act in accord with His choices.

When you're stuck, you must be willing to examine exactly what is keeping you from moving forward. Could it be fear? The fear of success keeps a lot of people from living up to their full potential. Though they are not satisfied where they are, they are even more afraid of what success will require of them. This can apply to any area of life from career to love.

Be honest. Look around you. Where are you? Where would you like to go? What will you have to do to get there? What are you willing to sacrifice in order to reach your destination? How badly do you want what you want? What will holding on to the same old stuff eventually cost you?

Until your desire overrides your fear, you will be stuck. So face your fears. Determine that what you want is more important than your anxiety and go for it. Hang on to God's hand for support and claim the life you want.

Something to consider is why you want what you want. Sometimes selfishness can get us caught up in an endless quagmire. It is not until we get over ourselves and accept that life is not about us that we will be able to move on. Some people in life just blame everyone and everything but the real problem: themselves. Is everyone around you moving on? If so, you're the one with the problem.

When you purpose to become all that He designed you to be as opposed to creating your own blueprint, you will be free to build and decorate your life in ways that make you a wonderful oasis for others. That is when you will move beyond your present state to adding beautiful blessings and surprises to your existence. Remember, there will always be movement in your life when you are reaching out to others. Want to get out of your rut? Reach out your hand.

This day life and death, blessing and curses have been set before you along with the power to choose. Choose life and all it has to offer. Choose the Architect's Blueprint over your own. If you lack resources, enlist help. People love the opportunity to be a blessing. Watch for the salvation of the Lord. He will lead you and guide you to your destination.

> For whoever wants to save his life will lose it,
> but whoever loses his life for me will find it.
> —Matthew 16:25 NIV

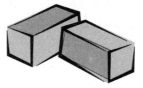

When life seems uncertain…

S ometimes it's hard to make sense out of life, especially if things have not gone according to plans. A new wife suddenly finds herself a widow, a man unexpectedly loses his job, a natural disaster destroys a person's home, someone is blindsided by betrayal, adultery, offense. All ask the same question: where does life go from here?

First of all, know that it is going somewhere. The issue becomes where you want it to go. Sometimes you simply don't know. Often at major turning points and transitions the Master Architect seems strangely silent on what to do next. This is a measure of protection, I am sure. If He revealed His plan too soon, we would surely mess it up, either by trying to help Him or by running ahead of Him.

When life seems uncertain, my advice is simple. I've said it before and I'll say it again: just trust God. Sounds simpler than it is, but do it anyway. If you don't know anything else about God, you know that He is faithful. Believe that He is still in control.

Next, keep doing what you are doing until it is clearly evident that you absolutely can't or shouldn't. Time will force life's hand and tell you when it is time to do something different. Stay tuned; say to God, "Cause me to hear Your lovingkindness in the morning, for in You do I trust; cause me to know the way in which I should walk, for I lift up my soul to You" (Ps. 143:8 nkjv). He will give direction.

Until then, know that this is what the walk of faith is all about: continuing on when you can't see the end, trusting that He who began a good work in you will be faithful to complete it (Phil. 1:6) and all things will work out for the good even though you can't make hide nor hair of sense out of things as they are (Rom. 8:28). This is when God is doing His best work.

What we must understand is that God does not owe us an explanation. He demands that we trust Him. So determined is He to complete His plans for us He works in spite of us. I recall my mother saying to me when I was a child, "That's all right—you don't have to like me now, you will like me later." Seeing the big picture of our lives, determined for us to grow up into the fullness of what He has designed, God will stop at nothing to finish His work in us. The circumstances are merely the tools He uses to refine us. The good, the bad, and the ugly all work together to build us up into what we ought to be.

When I was small I went on road trips with my parents. I was not certain of the details of how we would get to our destination. I couldn't read or understand the map or check our time frame. But they seemed pretty sure about where they were going. Sometimes I would complain that it was taking way too long for us to get there. I was tired. I wanted out of the car. But this did not make them stop. They just kept going. They had calculated the route and remained steadfast in their mission to reach our destination at the time they had estimated.

After growing weary and asking repeatedly, "Are we there yet?" I decided my time could be better spent either enjoying the scenery, occupying myself with a game, or taking a nap and letting them wake me up when we had finally reached our destination.

And so it is with life. When things are uncertain, let's face it: we are out of control and there is usually little, if anything, we can do. Any decision we make in our helpless state should not come from fear or desperation. If only we could see God not only as the Master Architect but as a loving parent who knows where we are going, perhaps we could let go enough to allow Him to drive. Then we can relax even when we don't know what's next. Resting in the arms of God we simply say, "Wake me up when we get there."

"For I know the plans I have for you," declares the Lord,
"plans to prosper you and not to harm you,
plans to give you hope and a future."
—Jeremiah 29:11 NIV

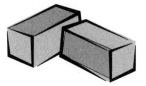

When life seems over...

The end, as we see it, is never the end of the matter. For those who believe as well as those who don't, life is eternal. Yet between eternity and the here and now are some painful cycles, some that nearly kill us emotionally and spiritually.

After the death of my boyfriend some years ago, I felt life was over. How could I live without this person who had become like breath to me? My emotional pain was so deep I could feel it physically, and I felt I had nowhere to turn.

Each day seemed interminable. I lived for the night to claim me in sleep and hated when the sun arose to wake me. I did not want to live, at least not without the man I loved.

And yet life was not over. I found new life as I cried out to God to help me. He visited me in my grief and gave me new reasons for living.

Usually we feel as if life is over when something that gave us life is taken away or leaves: a person, a career, a dream, a belief—anything that gave us a sense of power or significance or love. In truth, the only thing that should give us life is God. Nothing else should have as much power over us or our will to live.

Perhaps you are grieving something today and are screaming, "But, Michelle, life is over for me! I will never be the same or love that way again. Right now, God is not enough for me."

I hear you. Honesty is good. God can take it on the chin. He loves you anyway. But what to do?

First, take the time to grieve your loss. Don't let it go on interminably, but take some time. It is healthy to cry, to process your pain, to feel it and squeeze it until you grow weary of it. Then rest. Stop talking about it. Let silence do its work in healing.

Release; forgive; do whatever you have to do to let go. Make a date for moving on. Make plans for what your move will entail. Whether it will be geographic or mental, map it out. Enlist help to get you moving. Begin to look around you and find reasons to celebrate being alive. Decide to live and not die. Journal how you're feeling and list the revelations you receive during this time. (If you simply can't get beyond your pain, seek professional help. There are skillful people who can gently guide you back to life.)

When you are in pain, your mind is more sensitive, so take note of any special thoughts about yourself, about God, about others, about your situation. Write them down, then reread what you write. Decide, based on facts, not feelings, what is true and what is not. Then rewrite the parts that are wrong and not life-giving.

Begin to chronicle a list of things to be grateful for no matter how simplistic. The list will grow. And then allow time to do its work. Celebrate a good day, acknowledge a bad day, and look forward to the next good day. Take one day at a time until you can see the light at the end of the tunnel.

If you work with your pain and refuse to be swallowed by it, you will see and embrace life again. You will even run toward it, acknowledging that life was truly not over, you were just asleep. And then, with eyes wide open, you will see more reasons to live than ever before.

> Find rest, O my soul, in God alone;
> my hope comes from him.
>
> —Psalm 62:5 NIV

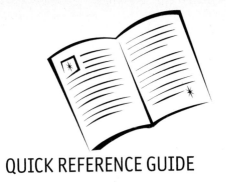

QUICK REFERENCE GUIDE

1. You get one life here on Earth, so build well.
2. You will give account for the life you build on Earth, so build with eternity in mind.
3. No one will ever care more about your life than you and God, so don't make it anyone else's responsibility.
4. Kill the fantasy that life is not supposed to be hard and accept the fact that it is.
5. Life doesn't just happen. You have to plan your work and work your plan.
6. Life has to have a firm foundation in order to stand the test of time.
7. It is not the sum total of what you acquire in life but the life you give to others that will define you.
8. Choose wisely—your life depends on it.
9. Life is an adventure—decide to enjoy it.
10. Life isn't life until you give it away.
11. Never attempt to assemble or maintain life without God.

CUSTOMER SERVICE

Running throughout this manual is a subtle theme. In life, you get what you give. Therefore, customer service begins with you. In the Master Architect's Blueprint, He states, "For even the Son of Man [Jesus] did not come to be served, but to serve, and to give his life as a ransom for many" (Mark 10:45 NIV). As you seek to serve others, you will be served: "He who refreshes others will himself be refreshed" (Prov. 11:25 NIV).

When you pour into others' lives, you receive the fulfillment of knowing that you made significant contributions to others' well-being—and that is the most life-giving thing you can do.

Your life, when it's working, can feed so many other lives. Share it.

TECH SUPPORT

"The Counselor, the Holy Spirit...will teach you all things and will remind you of everything I have said to you" (John 14:26 NIV).

- ✢ For help on any life issue, dial 1-800-12-JESUS.
- ✢ The operator will put you right through.
- ✢ There will be no computer prompts. Your call will not be put on hold.
- ✢ Your questions will be answered in a timely and effective manner.
- ✢ For quality assurance purposes, your call will be recorded in heaven.
- ✢ If further assistance is needed, a ministering angel along with earthly counsel will be dispatched to you immediately.

After receiving instruction, please refer to the Manufacturer's Blueprint and follow the directions to ensure a long-lasting, high-quality working life.

WARRANTY INFORMATION

Your warranty offers several beneficial perks:

> Roadside Assistance Anywhere
> Life Protection Plan
> Believer's Assurance Plan
> Accident Insurance
> Health Renewal Plan
> Disaster Relief Insurance*
> Flexible Coverage Policy—Tailored to your specific needs
> Global Assist Program

*There is no fine print.

PLEASE NOTE THAT THIS WARRANTY IS ISSUED BY INVITATION ONLY. THOSE WHO RSVP TO THE MASTER ARCHITECT BECOME IMMEDIATE RECIPIENTS OF ALL PROVISIONS. IF YOU ARE A CONSUMER ON ANY CONTINENT IN THE WORLD, THIS WARRANTY IS FOR YOU. IT HAS NO TERRITORIAL RESTRICTIONS OR EXPIRATION DATE. (In other words, it's honored everywhere throughout eternity, as life never ends.)

BLUEPRINT: Heaven Inc., warrants to the original user that the Master Architect's Blueprint is free from defects in workmanship, is complete, and is perfectly reliable.

EXCLUSIONS: This warranty excludes any design, addition, or structure that is not part of the Master Architect's Blueprint.

OBTAINING WARRANTY SERVICE: Simply refer back to the Manufacturer's Blueprint (the Bible). This will keep life working smoothly. When in doubt, seek counsel from a source trained by the Master Architect.

WARRANTY EXCLUSIVE: Either you believe God's promises or you don't. The only way this warranty will expire is if you choose to stop believing. Because of the power of the Master Architect, know that anytime you run out of power or wisdom, He is your life, He is all you need, and you can rest in Him. He will give you the strength to continue. The warranty remains active and is available for touch-ups, additions, and renovations ad infinitum.

LIMITATION OR LIABILITY: The Master Architect knows no limits. When you are working in direct relationship with Him, all things are possible, no matter how much wear and tear your life is subjected to. The lives He builds and maintains are guaranteed to keep working and stay beautiful if they adhere to His instructions as detailed in the Blueprint. If left to the discretion of the user, life may not work at all.

DISCLAIMER: If decisions are not initiated or approved by the Master Architect or His Blueprint, the dysfunction life sustains will be on you.

About the Author

Michelle McKinney Hammond is a bestselling author, speaker, relationship expert and empowerment coach, singer/songwriter, and television cohost. She is known for blending a refreshing femininity with hard-hitting reality checks. She has written more than twenty-nine books, including *How to Make Love Work* and *The DIVA Principle,* as well as the bestselling titles *Sassy, Single & Satisfied, Secrets of an Irresistible Woman,* and *101 Ways to Get and Keep His Attention.* For more information or to contact Michelle McKinney Hammond, you can visit her Web site at www.michellehammond.com or write to:

HeartWing Ministries
PO Box 11052
Chicago, IL 60611